The Long Climb

One Man's Journey from Addiction to Faith

Robert Woods, PhD

MADE FOR SUCCESS

Made for Success Publishing
www.MadeForSuccess.com

Distributed by Made for Success

First Printing
Library of Congress Cataloging-in-Publication data
Woods, Robert, PhD
The Long Climb: One Man's Journey from Addiction to Faith
p. cm.

LCCN: 2025943992
ISBN: 978-1-64146-963-0 *(pbk)*
ISBN: 978-1-64146-964-7 *(eBook)*
ISBN: 978-1-64146-965-4 *(audio)*

Printed in the United States of America

For further information, contact Made for Success Publishing
email *service@madeforsuccess.net.*

The Long Climb is an incredible story of perseverance; however, it includes elements that might not be suitable for all readers, such as sexual abuse, drug and alcohol abuse, and suicidal ideation.

To Robert, my eleven-year-old self. You were not a bad kid doing bad things. You were a kid in distress, crying out for help. I believed in you then, and I believe in you now. Be the light for all of those who live in darkness.

Contents

Foreword ix
Introduction.................................. xi
Chapter One: My Father's Presence 1
Chapter Two: Where's Dad?......................... 12
Chapter Three: Dad is Gone......................... 21
Chapter Four: Hell................................ 26
Chapter Five: Glimmers of Hope 42
Chapter Six: The Last Straw 51
Chapter Seven: Bicycle Racing 61
Chapter Eight: Love, Marriage, and Addiction............ 77
Chapter Nine: Recovery........................... 105
Chapter Ten: GED to PhD 125
Chapter Eleven: More Doubt than Faith 139
Chapter Twelve: Let Go and Let God.................. 150
Chapter Thirteen: From Prison to Prison 170
Chapter Fourteen: A Badge of Honor.................. 180
Chapter Fifteen: Back on the Bike 196
Chapter Sixteen: Life after Trauma................... 206
Acknowledgments 212
About the Author................................ 214

Foreword

In the realm of human endeavor, few pursuits test the limits of persistence and determination as profoundly as ultra-endurance events. These grueling challenges—whether spanning deserts, mountains, or endless open roads—demand not just physical strength but an unyielding spirit, a relentless drive to push beyond what seems possible. It is in this extraordinary arena that Robert has carved his legacy, and it is his remarkable journey that this book so vividly captures.

Robert's story is not merely one of athletic feats, though his accomplishments in ultra-endurance events are nothing short of awe-inspiring. It is a testament to the power of the human will, a narrative woven with moments of triumph, struggle, and profound self-discovery. Through the pages of this book, you will walk alongside a man who has faced the unrelenting trials of body and mind, who has stared down doubt and exhaustion, and who has emerged, time and again, with a renewed sense of purpose.

What sets Robert`apart is not just his ability to endure but his unwavering commitment to chasing high-level goals that most would deem unattainable. His journey reminds us that true success is not measured solely by crossing finish lines but by the courage to keep moving forward when every fiber of your being begs you to stop. Each step, each mile, each moment of perseverance has shaped not only Robert's character but also the inspiration he offers to others.

This book is more than a chronicle of races run, or personal records set; it is a window into the heart of a man who embodies resilience, who shows us that the pursuit of greatness is a marathon, not a sprint. As you turn these pages, may you find yourself inspired by Robert's indomitable spirit, challenged to reflect on your own aspirations, and emboldened to chase your dreams with the same tenacity that has defined his extraordinary path.

With admiration,
Scott Proscia, BS ATC M.Ed
Head Performance Coach
VIP Endurance Racing
www.vipenduranceracing.com

Introduction

I was a high school dropout with a chip on my shoulder and nothing to lose. I was addicted to any substance that crossed my path, and I was a father of four by the time I was twenty-two. How I raised my boys as a single dad with sole custody, overcame addiction, became a licensed New York State Education Supervisor with a PhD, and developed into an accomplished endurance athlete is nothing short of a miracle. A guy like me should have ended up either dead or in prison. Instead, I share my story to inspire those with nothing to lose. Because when you have nothing to lose, you have everything to gain.

I failed the seventh and the ninth grades, was expelled from high school, and began having problems with the law. So, my alcoholic father decided I should live with him, thinking that would be the solution. Running away from home at fifteen, I did not go back until my dad got sober, and I had nothing left. My father's love allowed me to experience a full life when I was headed for a life filled with emptiness and self-destruction.

My transformation began when my dad helped me get into a drug and alcohol rehabilitation center. I spent eighteen months there. While in treatment, I completed my GED, and I realized school was a bridge to a new life full of opportunities. I applied to an educational program, the Adult Education Program and Policy (AEPP), and was accepted. They paid for one full-time semester of college. Acceptance into this program was all the inspiration I needed to commit to and pay for the rest of my educational journey.

Soon after I was successfully discharged from the treatment center, my ex-wife asked me to take custody of our four boys. There was no other answer but "yes." I was now a single dad. I worked a full-time job and had no idea how I'd manage it all. But with God's help and help from those who loved me, I did.

As you can imagine, having to take my young children with me to school meant that things didn't always go as planned. My boys usually sat in the hall doing their homework outside my college classrooms while I attended class, though they occasionally made an appearance in the classroom. We still laugh about those experiences.

Over the years, I completed several college programs. I received an AS in human services, a BA in education, an MS in reading, an advanced degree (CAS) in educational leadership, and a PhD in educational leadership. I went from hating school to becoming an educator.

My passion and my gifts have always been to help troubled souls through education. The miracles that happened kept me going when the pressure of being an administrator in a high-stress environment made me want to resign. They also inspired me to share my experience with the world. Life's hardships only make sense when we use them to help others. Otherwise, the hardships are in vain.

In addition to getting clean and sober, getting educated,

and becoming an educator, Jesus my Shepherd brought me to the flock. It began with my mother and stepfather taking me to church. I found comfort there. My faith has grown and continues to grow since then.

Physically I went from three hundred pounds to one hundred and ninety. I had always been active, but after an unexpected neck surgery, my active life screeched to a halt. I was devastated. I ate more than I should. Only God could have known the depth of the pain in my heart. And He knew my process to a new life in Him could not be rushed. Little by little, through small miracles, I began to trust Him.

I began my journey back to health by training for various marathons and endurance events. I am faced with a lot of naysayers who think I'm crazy. But my personal pursuits guide me into the depths of my being and help me to become the best human being possible including using my gifts to help others. My dear friend, Very Rev. Fr. Maduawuchi S. Ogbonna, CSSP, PhD (Father Stan), an Igbo from South-Eastern Nigeria and Roman Catholic Priest, reminds me often that I cannot harbor my gifts, or my story, and I must share them with the world.

Now that I have retired from public service, have an endurance platform, and a very strong faith, I want to provide hope and healing for people who have suffered trauma and abuse, people who have nothing to lose. I want to show them that it is possible to heal and overcome. That it is possible to achieve their dreams.

After many hours in deep conversation about the direction of my life with Fr. Stan, one day, I asked him, "Father, what is my Igbo name?"

He said, "Chukwuemeka. It means 'God has done so much.'"

I looked at him, smiled, and said, "My Igbo name is a perfect match. God has done so much for me."

He put his hand on my shoulder and added, "Robert, you cannot harbor your story. You must share it with the world. It is His story."

I nodded my head in agreement. "I will, Father. But I don't understand God's Grace and why he has helped me while others still struggle."

Without hesitation, Father exclaimed, "There is no redemption without permission!"

This explanation made perfect sense. In my recovery circle, we have a slogan when we see someone who is in the grips of addiction. We say, "But for the Grace of God, there go I." It is through the grace of God that I got clean and sober. When God's Grace is present, we have the choice to say yes. And I have been saying yes for a long time.

CHAPTER ONE

My Father's Presence

"The quiet presence of a father gives strength and security, a foundation upon which we build our dreams."

- Unknown

When I was young, I loved being the first one up in the morning. There was a quietness that I found pleasant and comforting. I could hear the subtle noises that were drowned out during the day: the refrigerator running, the furnace clanking, the willow tree branches tapping at the side of the house. I heard morning creatures like frogs and toads. I often wondered if they were talking to each other or if they just liked making noise, letting everything and everybody know they existed.

It was the summer of 1973 about an hour north of New York City. My favorite player was Bobby Murcer. He played center field for the New York Yankees. The Yankees had not won a World Series since 1962 against the Los Angeles Dodgers, two years before I was born, but I didn't care. I was a true pin-striped New York Yankees fan.

On this day, I got up extra early. In a matter of hours, I would be going to a New York Yankees game with my dad and brothers. Who could sleep knowing they were going to see their favorite baseball team play?

I sat up in bed and slipped on my fuzzy green slippers. They had soft, white fur inside and made my feet happy. I looked over at the bed against the opposite wall, where my younger brother JoÚ was sound asleep. I looked around our room, contemplating waking him up or not. There was a sewing table between our beds that we used as a nightstand. It had a hole in it for the sewing machine. We often used that hole as a basketball rim and played many games of Nerf basketball in our room.

After a moment, I decided to let JoÚ sleep. My plan was to sneak down to the end of the hallway, slip into my big brother Ben's room, and wake him up instead. I knew he was as excited as I was to go to the game, only he hated getting up early. He'd get angry when somebody woke him up. That day, I didn't care, though. I could not contain my excitement.

My biggest fear was waking up my mom and dad. Their room was right across the hallway from JoÚ and me—a bad location for us. I knew if I woke them up, they would be livid. The trick was to tiptoe down the hallway without creaking the hardwood floor. I hated those floors for two reasons: it was almost impossible to sneak down the hallway without getting caught, and without fail, sometime during the day or night, when I forgot to put on my slippers, I'd wind up with a splinter in my foot. My mom would inevitably have to get the needle and dig it out.

Luckily, I managed to make it down the hallway with

soft enough creaks so as not to wake up my parents. I snuck into my brother's room, where he was sound asleep, snoring away.

Ben's room was neat and orderly. My dad had let us pick the color schemes of our rooms. Ben's room was blue and silver like the Dallas Cowboys, while JoÚ and I had picked green and yellow, the colors of the Green Bay Packers. On his desk, he had several model cars he had built. He'd lay out each part separately, paint each part, let them dry, and then assemble the model. I saw it as a waste of time. Just give me a car that's already put together so I can play with it.

I entered Ben's room and picked up each of his models to observe them closely. He'd never let me do that if he were awake, so I took advantage of the opportunity. His closet was set up with all his G.I. Joe stuff. I peeked in there, but it was too dark to see clearly. I thought it best to leave G.I. Joe alone. Finally, I couldn't stand it any longer, so I started pushing Ben's shoulder and whispered, "Ben, wake up. Wake up!"

I wasn't prepared for his outburst. He sat up quickly, making me jump back. He screamed, "Get out! Get out! Go back to bed! It's too early in the morning to be up!"

I ran as fast as I could back to my room, not caring about the floor creaking or catching a splinter. I sat on my bed, breathing heavily, sorry to have made the choice to wake up Ben. I was just thinking that I should have known better when my door crept open, and my mom peeked in. "Robert, go back to sleep. You're going to wake up everyone in the house."

There was no way I was going back to sleep. It was light enough outside for me to see. When she left, I retrieved my imitation Bobby Murcer ball glove, put my face in it, and breathed in the sweet smell of leather. I loved the smell of that glove. I spit into it and rubbed it into my glove, a trick of the trade my father taught me. I treasured the little tips my dad offered me on sports. I crawled under my bed, looking for the hard ball I had lost several days prior. Luckily, I found it. I took the ball and threw it into my glove over and over. I just knew that one day, I would be playing for the New York Yankees. I imagined I was warming up, about to play third base. I knew exactly how they warmed up because of all the baseball games I'd watched on TV with my family.

I tiptoed down the stairs. My dad had put stair carpeting down the middle of the stairs, so I walked on the carpet to soften my footsteps. My Saturday morning chore was to take a bucket of soapy water and clean the sides of each stair. I hated that chore and did whatever it took to get out of it. I didn't have much luck convincing my parents to give me a pass; I hoped they would today. I made it to the bottom of the stairs, but opening the French door without making noise was complicated. It was a beautiful door with fifteen individual windows arranged in five rows of three. Mom loved it. She had made beautiful curtains for it, which she tied back in the day and let down at night. I unlocked the door and quietly opened it, slipping out into the driveway. I was free!

I found my pitchback, a net attached to springs fastened on a stand. It was an apparatus that allowed someone to throw a ball at it, and it would pitch it back—hence, pitchback. I set it up in the front yard and threw my hardball at it. The harder I threw the ball, the faster it returned. I loved it. When I got tired of the pitchback, I threw the ball into the air as high as I could and made the catch. It felt like I was only out there for ten minutes, but I must have lost track of time because I heard my mom yell, "Robert Heine, it's time for breakfast!"

I was hungry for sure. My stomach growled. But if I had my choice, baseball or breakfast, I would have chosen to continue playing baseball.

My mom yelled again, "Robert, you know you are going to a Yankees game today. Go get cleaned up and come down for breakfast."

I ran upstairs as fast as I could. I washed my hands and face and scurried downstairs to the kitchen table. The kitchen was huge and received the most traffic. There were four doorways leading into the dining room, the living room, the back porch, and the downstairs hallway. My mom had sewn curtains for the kitchen windows. She was always sewing. The humming of her Singer invariably reminded me of home. In the center of the room, my dad had placed a large round table. Above the table, an adjustable light fixture illuminated the space with a warm glow.

I entered the kitchen, and my mom had four plates and silverware all set up. JoÚ was already seated at the table. Ben was still sleeping. Ben would sleep into the afternoon if my parents let him. My mom stood in front of the stove, tending to the bacon.

The pressure cooker started to hiss. The sound gave me a sense of security. It meant I was fed and cared for. My mom always had a pot of pinto beans on the stove. One time, I stopped the little gadget on top of the pressure cooker from making the hissing sound. My mom flew around the corner and slapped my hand away hard enough to make me cry. She screamed, "Don't you ever do that again! The cooker could explode!" I gave my mom a good scare on that one. I can't ever hear a pressure cooker without thinking of that day.

While Mom was tending to the bacon, the washing machine started to dance all over the kitchen. If the clothes were off balance, the machine had a mind of its own. It didn't bother any of us; we were used to it.

I jumped onto a chair, nearly knocking my little brother out of his seat, and slammed the ball and glove on the table. My mom always had a tablecloth covering the table. Like clockwork, whenever JoÚ was seated at the table, I would give the tablecloth a tug and make JoÚ's plate fly up into the air. Today, he was poised and ready to tattle on me.

JoÚ yelled, "Mom, Rob pulled on the tablecloth!"

"Robert Heine! How many times do I have to tell you to stop pulling on the tablecloth?"

I hated it when my mom called me Robert Heine. I got my middle name from my dad's friend, Heine. They met in Sioux Falls, South Dakota, where I was born. My middle name is pronounced just like the word for butt, heinie. My brother and sister always teased me with sarcastic voices, "Hey Rob, say high to your knee" or "Hey Rob, are you going to sit on your heinie?" I'd run away feeling like I could explode.

I looked at my brother with an ear-to-ear smile and yanked the cloth again, sending his plate high into the air. Just as he was about to tattle on me again, my mom grabbed my plate and placed bacon, eggs, home fries, and two pieces of toast on it. She set my plate down in front of me, with an exhausted look. "How many times do I have to tell you not to bring that glove to the table? Take it outside now!"

JoÚ laughed. I grabbed my glove and gave my brother a shoulder bump, trying to knock him out of his chair. I stomped down the hallway and out the front door, putting my glove and ball on the front step.

I heard my dad coming down the stairs, calling out, "What's going on down here?"

My mom replied, "Rob keeps picking on his brother and brought his ball and glove to the table again."

My dad looked at me with a grin. "Son, leave your brother alone and stop bringing that glove to the table."

I could tell he was proud of the fact that I loved baseball as much as he did. He'd once aspired to become a professional baseball player.

My dad brought strength to our household. He didn't have to say much; his presence did the talking. He gave each of us subtle confidence to face the challenges of our daily lives. I grinned at him as I returned to the breakfast table. I looked up to him as a man, hoping that one day, I could be just like him.

I plopped back down into my chair and began eating my breakfast. The washing machine had finally stopped dancing. I neatly piled my eggs and bacon on a piece of toast and then placed the other piece of toast on top of it, pushing down as hard as I could. I always made my food into a sandwich, even my dinners.

"Eat a good breakfast. It's going to be a long day. I packed a snack bag for you boys to take to the game," my mom suggested in a loving voice.

My mom was sensational. She was short in stature but

a giant in disposition and still is to this day. At the time, she only stood four feet ten inches tall and had curly brown hair in the shape of an afro. She wore cat glasses, the style in the 1970s, and every day, without fail, an apron. My mom was tough as nails and knew how to manage a house with kids. She could cook, sew, wash clothes, and discipline kids all at the same time, never skipping a beat. We all knew better than to give her a hard time, but I just couldn't help messing with JoÚ.

My dad had built a clothesline for her, so she didn't have to leave the kitchen to hang clothes. It was attached to the back of the house and a tree about twenty yards from the house. It seemed to be the length of a football field. It had pulleys so my mom could stand in one spot while hanging clothes. I loved the sound of the clothesline pulleys. They squeaked and comforted me. I heard that sound, and I thought of my family and how happy we all were to be together.

After I wolfed down my breakfast, I sat back while my mom hung clothes, feeling like the luckiest kid on the planet. My mom and dad were happy and smiling most of the time, and today, I got to go to the New York Yankees game with my brothers. I hoped to see Bobby Murcer and my other favorite player, Roy White. I planned to bring my glove, hoping to catch a foul ball. My dad had told us the day before to bring our gloves and be prepared to catch foul balls—and I always listened to my dad when it came to sports. I wanted to make him proud of me. I dreamed that Bobby Murcer would hit a foul ball, and I would make an amazing catch. Then, Bobby would look for me after the game and say, "Hey, kid! Nice catch! Come here. I'll autograph your ball."

When my dad finished his breakfast, he declared in his deep, southern drawl, "All right, boys, get your stuff. We are leaving." Even when he said simple things like that, I loved to hear him talk.

My brothers and I raced to the car, a blue 1970 Ford LTD. Being older, Ben always got the front seat, leaving JoÚ and me stuck in the back seat.

My dad made sure we were all buckled up and quipped, "Y'all have your ball gloves?"

At the same time, we nodded and replied, "Yes!"

JoÚ loved to roll his window down and up again and again. JoÚ kept messing with the window until my dad commanded, "JoÚ, roll it up or down and leave it alone."

JoÚ chose down. I rolled mine down, too, because I liked putting my face in the open space and letting the wind make my eyes water. JoÚ and I got comfortable and rolled my hard ball back and forth to each other most of the way there.

I'd never been to New York City. I was so excited about going to a Yankees game that I did not think too much about the trip itself. Suddenly, the trip became much more than just going to a baseball game. The world became a much larger place, and my dad became my anchor. I watched the familiar countryside fade into more and more buildings. I noticed buses, taxicabs, and trains. The comfort of my small-town upbringing left me, and I began to feel uncomfortable. I looked at a high-rise apartment building and wondered how many families lived in it. I tried to imagine what it would be like to live in a building like that without a front and back yard. I got an up-close look at a city bus driver and wondered why he would want to drive a bus all over a big city. It scared me to even think about it. Before I could process my thoughts, a police car went flying past us with its siren on. I had never seen a car go so fast. Each new encounter started to make me feel more anxious and scared. I felt like I wanted my dad to turn the car around and go home.

But as my fear started to grow, my dad said, "Hey boys, look over there. That is Yankee Stadium."

I assumed he must have been to the city before because none of the hustle and bustle of city life seemed to bother him. The sound of my father's voice calmed my fear and anxiety. I came back to the moment and to the reason we were there: to go see the New York Yankees.

"Dad, do you think I'll catch a Bobby Murcer foul ball?" I asked.

"Son, I certainly hope so!"

When we entered the stadium, my dad stopped at a souvenir booth to buy a program. He explained to us that in the center of the program, there would be a place to score the game. "When I was a boy, we didn't have television. I would listen to the radio and keep a scorebook of all the New York Yankees' games. I'll show y'all how to score a game when we get to our seats."

We left the souvenir stand, and my dad said with strong confidence, "Take my hand and stay close to me."

I reached out and grabbed his hand. At that moment, I knew that nothing would ever harm me. I was in the presence of my father.

Around 1972. Sitting with my dad's mom, my Grammie. I'm sitting next to her in a tan shirt.

CHAPTER TWO

Where's Dad?

"Boys want to grow up to be like their male role models. And boys who grow up in homes with absent fathers search the hardest to figure out what it means to be male."

- Geoffrey Canada

It was 1976. The Dallas Cowboys lost to the Pittsburgh Steelers in the Super Bowl. A month prior, my dad jumped up and hit his head on the ceiling when Drew Pearson caught a Hail Mary pass from Roger Staubach to win against the Minnesota Vikings in the playoffs. I stared at my brothers with a look of disbelief as I watched the dust sprinkle down from the ceiling. I thought, "That's the coolest thing I've ever seen."

I loved football as much as I loved baseball. My dad and older brother were Dallas Cowboys fans. I liked the Green Bay Packers, and my younger brother liked the Cleveland Browns. Secretly, I liked the Dallas Cowboys, too, but I enjoyed being different. My favorite player on the Cowboys was their fullback, Robert Newhouse. A fullback runs the ball for short-yardage gains and must be super strong with powerful legs. I was built like Robert Newhouse, short and stocky with enormous thigh muscles, and we shared the same name. He basically tried to run through and run over the defensive players. It often took several players to tackle Robert, just like it would take several of my friends to tackle me.

During football season, I lived and breathed the game. I forgot about baseball and went all in with football. My dad used to take the time to teach my brothers and me football plays—specifically, timing plays. He called them patterns. The receiver (the player who catches the ball) would run a specific pattern, and the quarterback (the player who throws the ball) would recognize the pattern and throw the ball, timing the pass with the receiver's pattern. Dad taught us four patterns, and we called them A, B, C, and D. I loved it, and it made sense to me. Every football season, my dad would be out in the front yard with me and my brothers, refining our football skills and working on our patterns.

However, this year was different. My dad worked late and wasn't around much on the weekends. I felt guilty as if it was my fault. I knew his absence must have been because he was disappointed with me. I told myself that I would do my chores better, be more helpful to my mom, and not pick on JoÚ as much. I didn't want my dad to be mad or disappointed with me.

Even though my dad wasn't around as much, it didn't stop my brothers and me from playing football. Ben continued developing our patterned plays. If it was just Ben and me, we would play against each other. We called it one-on-one football. Our front yard wasn't the perfect field for playing football; it was wide, then skinny, and wide again, but we made it work. I felt grateful to have a brother like Ben. He was my brother and my best friend.

Football was amazing because it unleashed my inner warrior. I loved carrying the football. Running back and fullback were my two favorite positions; both required that once I got the ball, I ran powerfully to the end zone. I would tuck the ball securely under my arm, and instantly, I transformed into a superhero. I possessed the confidence to leap over tall buildings and run through brick walls. It was magical. I always wanted more of it.

I knew my dad noticed something special about me because he gave me inspirational talks and shared the wisdom of his football coaches with me. I felt sad that Dad wasn't around anymore to watch me develop into a powerful running back and to give me those little pep talks. I felt confused and continued to blame myself for his absence. I wrote an essay for school describing how I planned to follow everything my dad told me about becoming a professional football player. I looked up to my dad and trusted him. I wished he was around more.

One day, instead of playing football, Ben and my sister, Mary Alice, wanted to go to the local playground, and of course, I did, too.

"Rob, come on. Ben and I are leaving!" my sister yelled.

"Alright, I'm coming. I have to find my football!" I yelled back. As soon as I found it, we took off for the playground.

My mom called after us, "Y'all be careful and look out for Rob."

My sister assured her that they would.

On the way to the playground, I tossed the football up in the air, playing self-catch all the way there.

Occasionally, Ben enthusiastically cheered, "Rob, throw me a pass." He'd run ahead, and I'd pass him the ball.

It was a short walk to the playground. Most of the neighborhood kids hung out there, so we always hoped to see some of them. My sister loved the swing set, and Ben and I loved the merry-go-round. The big metal slide never got any attention. Either it was too hot or too slow and sticky to slide down.

When we arrived at the playground, my sister went directly for the swings, and Ben and I went for the merry-go-round. We got that thing to spin faster and faster.

Ben beamed, "Jump off, lay down, and close your eyes!"

I don't know why I listened to him. I got dizzy and almost threw up. That was the point, but I didn't like the feeling. It was the same feeling I got when I saw blood or got seriously hurt. I never liked to feel woozy on purpose.

After a few hours at the playground, we were ready to leave.

"Let's take the trail home," Ben suggested. The trail led right to our backyard. I never liked to take the trail alone. When I did, it always felt like someone was following me. Unafraid, Ben and Mary Alice crossed the road and waited at the beginning of the trail.

Mary Alice grumbled, "Rob, hurry up, or we are going to leave you here!"

"Alright!" I whined. "I forgot my football."

I grabbed my football and took off running. Instead of taking the staircase in their direction, I took a shorter route. I jumped off a stone wall that led to the trail. Unfortunately, I landed on a broken coke bottle. The bottle's jagged edge caught me in the left leg and left a gaping wound. I screamed as loud as I could, and they knew I wasn't kidding. They ran over to me and saw my leg and all the blood. Both of their faces turned white.

Mary Alice said, "We need to get him home now."

I started to panic and got that woozy feeling, the same feeling I got jumping off the merry-go-round not long ago. I felt dizzy and lightheaded. Ben and Mary Alice helped me home as fast as they could, trying not to hurt me. My mother heard me screaming and came running from behind her black Singer sewing machine. She grabbed a blue bath towel and held it on my leg. It turned from blue to red almost immediately.

"We're going to the Emergency Room. You're going to need some stitches!" my mom declared.

She was used to it. I had been stitched up multiple times. Plus, she'd taken nursing classes in college and had some medical experience. She calmed me down and assured me I would be okay.

My sister looked over at me, and our eyes met. She looked pale. Ben stood next to her with a blank stare on his face. They both knew it was a pretty serious injury. I felt bad for them because they would feel guilty even though it was my fault. I thought, "I should have taken the staircase." I could tell by the looks on their faces that they loved me and hoped I would be okay. I felt grateful to have them as my brother and sister.

Ben and Mary Alice quietly disappeared into their rooms. My sister, more than my brother, probably felt like she was in big trouble since she was responsible for looking out for me. But my mom didn't have time for disciplining or consoling them. She had to stay focused on getting me to the Emergency Room. My dad raced home from work, and the three of us took off, leaving my sister in charge again.

On the way to the ER, I thought about all the trips I had made there. The first serious injury occurred a few months prior to this one. I had been playing basketball in my room with Ben. The ball hit the lightbulb cover, causing the cover to fall and land right on top of my head. I didn't even feel pain, but when I felt the blood trickle down the side of my face, I knew there was a problem and screamed bloody murder. That incident resulted in ten stitches on top of my head.

On another occasion, I was playing Army with my brother Ben and his friend when I was hit in the head with a brick. It resulted in seventeen stitches in my head. It seemed like I was the only one who ever got hurt.

Another time, we played hide and go seek, and I ripped open my hand on our dog's house. That one needed twelve stitches. The very next day, I got hit in the mouth with a kickball while eating ice cream, and the spoon cut my uvula, the thing that hangs in the back of the throat. That scared me worse than all the others. I felt like I couldn't breathe and wasn't sure how they were going to stitch my uvula, but they did it using dissolvable stitches.

After cutting my leg on the broken Coke bottle, we arrived at the hospital, and the overseeing doctor was the same one who had stitched me up on all the other occasions, Dr. Beauboff. He had a funny accent. When he saw my parents, he asked, "What did Wobby do now?" He took the towel off my leg and added, "Yep, I'll have to stitch Wobby up again."

This time, I set the record. I got twenty stitches.

The stitches in my leg did not slow me down. The next day, I was back on the football field with all my friends from the neighborhood. My leg was bandaged up well; I never thought about reinjuring it. Common sense would have said, "You better not go out on the football field. There are twenty stitches in your leg, and if you bust them, it's not going to be good." But I did not have common sense when it came to sports; I just wanted to play. All I thought about was carrying the football and making a long-run play or scoring a touchdown. I didn't have time to think about getting hurt. My competitive adrenaline took over my decisions.

My team had the ball first, and my friend was the quarterback. He said, "Rob, pitch right."

The play went off smoothly. I broke right, and he pitched me the ball for a run play. I made a long run, avoiding lots of tackles, and even broke away from a few. Walking back to the huddle, I noticed my dad coming toward us, yelling, "Rob, come up here right now!"

I told my friends I'd be right back, but they all knew my game was over. I walked toward my dad with my head down, more upset about not playing than anything else.

"What's the matter with you? Don't you know you have twenty stitches in your leg? You're out there playing football and could easily bust all those stitches!"

I had no words or excuses. I just looked down at the ground. On most occasions, my dad would grab my chin and say, "Look at me when I'm talking to you!" But today was different. He understood how difficult it was for me not to play.

He put his hand on my shoulder and said, "Go inside and wash up. I want your mom to look at your leg."

I shrugged my shoulders and moped all the way to the house, wishing I could still be playing in the game instead of going inside to see my mother.

I was so mad that I was injured. I felt powerless and helpless. I thought, "What does my dad care anyway? It's my leg. And besides, he's never around anymore." Recently, he was spending more time away from the house and I didn't know why.

I found my mom in her sewing room and trudged toward her. "Dad told me to find you and have you look at my leg. He's mad that I was playing football."

My mom slowly peeled the bandage back, trying not to hurt me or the bandage. She was great at it and had the momma's touch. I trusted my mom more than I did the doctors.

She said, "Robert, your leg looks fine. It's not red, and no stitches are busted, but you have to take it easy until it heals."

I'm not a good patient and could not wait for the stitches to come out. I always wanted what I wanted instantly.

My mom continued, "Go down to the living room, elevate your leg, and watch television. I'll be down in a little while to check on you."

Mom came down about an hour later. She sat next to me and pushed my long, curly hair out of my face. "Rob, your dad and I care about you, and we don't want to see you make your injury worse."

I looked at my mom and replied, "Why does Dad care? He is barely home, and when he is, he always seems mad. You guys aren't happy like you used to be. What did I do to make Dad so unhappy?"

With sadness in her eyes, my mom apologetically said, "Your dad loves you very much. He works a lot."

I looked away from my mom and stared at the ceiling. My heart ached. I wanted my dad and mom to be happy together. I wanted my dad to be home. I lay there thinking about it until I couldn't keep my eyes open. I drifted off to sleep, hoping that when I woke up, everything would be back to normal.

CHAPTER THREE

Dad is Gone

"His leaving wasn't about you. It was about him."

- Iyanla Vanzant

In 1976, the New York Knicks were my favorite basketball team. Walt "Clyde" Frazier was my favorite player, and Earl "The Pearl" Monroe was right behind him. Although I was short, stocky, and better suited to play baseball and football, I still loved to play basketball. I had a great jump shot. I could score from just about anywhere on the court. My dribbling skills were way above average. I practiced dribbling all the time, and my mom often yelled at me to stop dribbling the ball in the house. In my hometown, I played in an organized youth basketball league for a team called the Knicks. My older brother and his friend were on the team, too, though my younger brother was not old enough to play yet. Our coach referred to us as the New York Knickerbockers, not the Knicks. We had blue uniforms with gold trims with a glossy look. I loved my uniform.

My coach was great and taught me and my teammates

the fundamentals of basketball. He taught me what Dad had once spent time teaching me. I learned offensive plays, like give and go and the back door play. I learned defensive strategies like a man-to-man and a two-one-two defense. His practices were tough, but I loved every minute of them. Coach's practices kept me focused on excelling as an athlete and helped ease the pain of the stress at home.

I knew things at home had changed. I sensed a tension between my mom and dad that made me uneasy most of the time. Dad was rarely at home, leaving all the house responsibilities to my mom. My mom's pressure cooker rarely hissed anymore, her sewing machine hummed less, and the clothesline pulleys stopped squeaking. I badly wanted to know what was wrong or what I had done, but no one said anything. I was confused. My dad's absence left a hole in me and in our entire home. There was a void in all of us. In his absence, an inner voice started to harass me, whispering in my ear, "It's your fault he's not here," and "Why play sports? Your dad's not here to watch you." I had no idea where that voice came from or why it showed up, but I wished it would leave me alone.

My mom and dad did a great job of hiding their dislike for each other from all of us—until they could no longer hide it. One day, as usual, my dad did not come home from work on time. I asked Mom, "Where is Dad? How come he's not home yet?"

My mom replied with her standard answer, "He's working late again."

My mom must have been fuming inside but wanted to be strong for my siblings and me. She tried to hide the deep-rooted resentments that were building against my dad. I'm sure every time one of us asked, "Where's Dad?" it added fuel to the fire already burning. But my mom did her best to keep the house together and keep our routines going.

That night, my mom hollered, "Rob and JoÚ, it's time for bed. Get washed up and say goodnight!"

I said, "We're watching the *Flintstones*. Can we finish watching it?"

"Yes, but right to bed after it's over."

JoÚ and I finished watching our show, washed up, and said goodnight. Mom had a stern look on her face, and I could feel the negative energy emanating from her. She kissed us goodnight, and JoÚ and I raced up the stairs to our bedroom.

I pulled my green bedspread back like I always did and grabbed my basketball. I plopped into bed and held my orange basketball. I rolled the ball through my fingers like I was taking a jump shot. I tried to get it as close to the ceiling as I could without hitting it. I loved watching the ball spin and always made sure it was a perfect spin.

I looked over at JoÚ, who was already under his covers and almost asleep. "Do you think Dad hates us?"

JoÚ yawned, "No, Dad likes us."

I loudly replied, "Then how come he never comes home, and when he does, he's always mad at us?"

JoÚ mumbled, "I don't know. Maybe he just has bad days at work."

I kept shooting the ball to the ceiling, and JoÚ fell asleep within ten minutes. I felt sleep coming on and put the ball down, falling asleep soon after my brother did.

It must have been about two o'clock in the morning when I was startled awake by a loud bang. I was sure it was my mom and dad's bedroom door slamming, but I was too scared to peek out to confirm the noise.

I heard my dad yell, "Lola, get up and make me a plate of food. I'm hungry!"

My mom yelled back at him, "You should have come home for dinner if you were hungry. Make your own damn food!"

My dad yelled even louder, "Make my goddam food!"

Now, JoÚ was awake and started crying. Tears rolled down his face. "Rob, make them stop fighting."

I wanted to grab him and hold him and make him feel safe, but I was scared, too. I froze at that moment. I didn't know what to do or what to say.

Finally, I said, "JoÚ, come over here. We'll hide under my bed together."

I kept a yellow flashlight on my nightstand. I turned it on, and we both crawled under my bed. I worked the bedspread down along the edges of my bed so that it hung down enough to cover us up. I whispered, "Don't worry, JoÚ. No one can see us under here. We are safe."

JoÚ stopped crying, and we listened to Mom and Dad yell at each other. It felt like hours, but it was more like minutes. Mom and Dad's bedroom door slammed. It rattled the entire house.

JoÚ started crying again, and all I could do was say, "JoÚ, don't worry. We'll be okay."

My dad stomped down the hallway, and then he must have fallen down the stairs. We heard *thump, thump, thump, thump*. When the thumping stopped, the front door slammed, and we heard glass shatter. My dad had broken one of the windows on our French front door when he slammed it. Still, JoÚ and I lay under my bed in silence. We were both scared but relieved that my dad was gone.

My dad's car tires squealed as he drove off into the middle of the night. JoÚ put his face down into his arms and started sobbing.

I put my hand on his back. "It's okay now. Dad left."

I sat silently and wondered where my dad would go. I wondered why he was so mad. Then came a gentle knock on our bedroom door.

My mom opened the door and said, "Y'all can come out now. Your father's gone."

Little did I know that would be the last time my father would come home.

I wished my dad would have come into my room one day and said, "Son, I'm really going to miss playing ball with you and helping you with life's challenges, but your mom and I just can't get along. It has nothing to do with you, your brothers, or your sister."

But he never did. Instead, my mom came into our room a few weeks later and announced, "Your dad won't be coming home anymore."

CHAPTER FOUR

Hell

"The path to paradise begins in hell."

- Dante Alighieri

The sounds of mom's sewing machine, the clothesline pulley, and the pressure cooker disappeared. After my dad left, so did the structure of our family. My mom was no longer a housewife. She got a second-shift job working for the state. She was gone from the time we got home from school until midnight. My older sister was gone most of the time, too, and eventually moved out. My older brother, at thirteen, was responsible for babysitting me and my younger brother.

It was as if somebody had opened our front door and rolled in a grenade. My entire life exploded, and there was nothing I could do about it. The dining room, the highlight of our house, became a litter box for our cats. They urinated all over the green carpet my dad had put down. No one ever went in there anymore. It smelled horrible, and my dad's antique desk sported a pile of junk mail and anything else that didn't have a home. The well-kept bookshelves lining the perimeter of the room were no longer neat, and books were scattered on the floor; some were shoved on the shelf backward, and other bookshelves had been knocked over. It was now a war room.

There was no longer someone to make us do Saturday chores, so the rest of the house was not far off from the state of the dining room. One night, my mom came home from work at midnight, and the house was a disaster. There were dishes everywhere.

She woke us all up and said, "Didn't I tell you boys to have this house clean when I got home?"

I rubbed my face with my hands to wake up and nodded my head yes. My mom had this weird look on her face. Her eyes were pinched, and she wore a scowl that I had never seen. Her wrinkles were more pronounced. What startled me the most was the empty stare in her eyes. She was looking at me, but it seemed as if she wasn't there; it was as if she was somebody else.

Mom left our room and went downstairs, looking for dirty dishes. I felt uneasy and scared. I knew something was wrong. Every time my mom found a dirty dish, she took it to the kitchen sink and smashed it.

I heard my brother Ben scurry down the stairs. He yelled, "Mom, stop! I'll wash the dishes and clean the house. I'm sorry. I didn't have time to clean up."

I got up and went downstairs to see what was going on. I watched as my mother grabbed a jar of pickles from the kitchen table, went to the sink, and smashed it.

Ben jumped in front of her and pleaded, "Mom, stop! I'll make sure the house is clean."

My mom drifted into the living room without saying a word.

I stood there for a few minutes and watched my brother in disbelief. I was confused. He stayed up into the wee hours of the night, cleaning up the broken dishes, the pickle jar, and the rest of the house. Somehow, he managed to get up for school the next day. My mom never said a word about the incident, and neither did we.

Instead of looking forward to each day, I began to develop survival skills. I walked on eggshells and tried not to disappoint Mom. I wanted to make it through the day without controversy. She no longer seemed concerned about our needs and wants. She was tired most of the time from long hours at work, and it felt like we were always in the way.

One day, on the bus ride home from school, my brothers and I agreed to meet our friends at the school to play basketball. We got off the bus in town, just up the road from our house. We all ran home, dropped our books off at the house, grabbed something to eat, and took off to the basketball court. I practiced my dribbling all the way to the court.

When we got there, there were at least ten kids already there. It was an outdoor court equipped for a full-court game, with a basketball rim on each side of the court. The rims and backboards were attached to metal poles. When the ball hit the rim too hard, it made a loud clanging sound, almost like the sound of symbols in an orchestra band. The winning team always stayed on the court, and the kids who called "next" would replace the losing team. We played until it got too dark to see the ball.

When it was my team's turn, I dribbled the ball down the court and passed it to a friend, who took a shot. It bounced off the rim. I jumped to grab the rebound but landed on my ankle sideways. My ankle buckled, and I heard a pop. I stood up to continue playing but could hardly walk.

Ben was on the opposite team, and he quipped in baby-talk, "Rob, stop being a baby. We need you."

But I couldn't play; the pain was unbearable. "I can't play!" I screamed. "I'm going home."

Ben and his friends teased me and called me a big baby.

My face turned beet red, and I balled up my fists. "I'm not a baby. I can't even walk."

I limped over to the playground where my brother JoÚ was playing.

"JoÚ, I sprained my ankle. I'm going home," I told him.

Unconcerned, he replied, "Okay, I'll go home with Ben."

I made it to the stone stairs, the entrance and exit of the playground. I grabbed the rail and hopped down the stairs, one step at a time. When I got to the bottom of the stairs, an older man who frequented the basketball court waited for me. He must have seen me sprain my ankle.

The man was riding a dark green ten-speed bike with the handlebars flipped upside down. I had seen him at the basketball courts before but did not know his name. He was good at basketball and the only one in the neighborhood who could dunk the ball. His hair was braided in six rows, which I thought looked cool, and he'd rolled his right pant leg up to keep it from getting stuck in his chain.

He looked at me and said, "Hey, kid. I saw you sprained your ankle. I'll give you a ride home."

"No, thanks," I replied. "I'm okay. I can walk."

But he insisted. I sat on the top tube of his bike, and he rode me home, asking, "Where are your parents?"

I replied, "My dad doesn't live at home, and Mom works the afternoon shift."

He dropped me off at my front door and told me to elevate my foot and put ice on it. I thanked him and never thought more about it.

I went to the freezer and grabbed an ice tray. I twisted it sideways to loosen up all the ice. I love the crackling sound it made because it made me think of my mom putting ice cubes in our tea glasses. I grabbed a sock and dumped the ice cubes into it, then went to the living room and turned on our old black and white TV set. *I Love Lucy* was on—one of my favorite shows. I put my foot up on a couple of pillows and put the sock on my ankle. It provided some relief and reduced the swelling. I hesitated for a moment and thought, "I wish my mom were home and my dad were here to give me advice on working through a sprained ankle." I felt abandoned and rejected; my mom and dad no longer cared about me and didn't want me. Tears welled up in my eyes, and one or two slowly trickled down the side of my face. Then, I started to cry. I didn't fight the tears and kept thinking about how my dad had always told me what his coaches had told him to do, and now he was gone. I missed those talks, and I missed my dad. I wiped my tears away with the back of my hand and thought about how happy I used to be. I wondered why things had changed. I longed for things to go back to the way they were.

When Ben got home, he asked, "Rob, why did you let that guy give you a ride home on his bike?"

"What? I told him no. But he insisted on giving me a ride. And how did you know?"

He leaned forward and pointed his finger at me. "My

friends saw you. They said he is bad news and to stay away from him."

My eyes got watery again, and I could feel my face redden. Instead of crying this time, I got mad. I hollered at him, "I told the guy I didn't need a ride, but he would not take no for an answer!"

Ben yelled back, "Well, stay away from him!"

I loudly replied, "Okay, I will!"

The next day, we all got off the bus and walked down our driveway. As soon as we got into the house, Ben noticed something and said, "Rob, JoÚ, we are going to play a game. We are going to run out the back door and hide in the weeds."

JoÚ and I laughed and went along with it.

Ben whispered, "Pretend like we are hiding from a monster."

We followed Ben out the back door and took off running. Once we made it out of our backyard, it became all high weeds.

We got to the weeds, and Ben declared, "Okay, duck down, and I'll keep watch to make sure the monster doesn't see us."

Ben kept peeking through the weeds and finally told us, "Okay, the monster is gone. We can go back to the house."

He did the same thing the next day. Only this time, Ben suggested, "Hey guys, we are going to play the same game, but we can't hide in the same place. The monster will know we are there."

JoÚ and I both laughed, and Ben said, "We are going to hide over by the big tree."

The big tree was just up the road from our house. It was a hangout spot for my friends and me. Ben went out the back door of our house with JoÚ and I right behind him. We hid behind the tree while Ben kept peeking around the trunk.

Eventually, he looked over at us and whispered, "Okay, it's clear. We can go home now. The monster is gone."

On the third day, Ben encouraged us to hide again. "Hey, guys. We are going to play the game again today."

Only this time, JoÚ replied, "I don't want to play. I'm watching *Bugs Bunny*."

I concurred, "I'm tired of this game."

Ben huffed. "Fine, then don't play. I'll be back in a little while. I'm going to my friend Pat's house." And off he went.

JoÚ and I had no idea that we were not playing a game. Ben was trying to protect us and hide us from a real monster. After Ben left, JoÚ watched cartoons, and I decided to take a bath. I hated that we didn't have a shower. We had one of those big, deep iron-cast bathtubs.

I hollered, "JoÚ, I'm taking a bath. I'll be out in a little while."

He replied, "Okay, when is Ben coming home?"

"I don't know. Whenever he goes to Pat's, he usually comes home just before Mom gets home."

I filled the tub with water and put my hand in it to make sure it was not too hot. There was a silver hook and latch set up to lock the door. As usual, I put the hook inside the eyelet and climbed into the tub. Before I even began to wash myself, I got that eerie feeling that something was wrong. The hairs on my arm stood up, and I said out loud, "Whose out there?" But there was no response. Then, I noticed an envelope slide through the crack of the door and pop the hook out of the eyelet. I froze. I had nowhere to run. I wanted to scream but couldn't. It was like a bad dream with something coming after me, but I couldn't move. Before I even realized what was happening, the door opened, and there stood the guy who had given me a ride home on his bicycle. He closed the door and put the latch back in the eyelet. He saw me in the tub and had a creepy smile on his face.

He said, "Don't worry, I'm not going to hurt you as long as you do what I say."

I was too scared to do anything. He walked over to the tub and unzipped his pants. He took my hands and told me to play with his erect penis. I wanted to say no, but I was too frightened. I did what he asked me to do. Then, he told me to stand up. He put a knife to my throat and said, "If you ever tell anyone, I will kill you and your entire family."

I didn't say a word. Tears poured down the side of my face. He then demanded, "Bend over."

When it was over, he pulled away from me, pulled up his pants, and said, "Remember what I said."

I stood there in complete disbelief. I didn't understand what had just happened. I knew it was wrong. I felt awful and disgusting. I tried to convince myself that it never happened, but everything inside me turned black. I felt as if I was covered in dirt and filth. I tried washing myself again and again after he left, but the feeling of being dirty wouldn't leave me. The filth wouldn't come off. I didn't know what to do. I stood there dazed and numb.

I put my pajamas on and called to JoÚ, "I'm going to bed. Shut the TV off before you go to bed."

Unaware of what had just happened, he called back, "Okay, I will."

I lay in bed that night, unable to sleep. I tried not to

think about it, but I couldn't. I kept replaying the scene over and over in my head. I kept asking myself, "Why didn't you jump out of the tub and run and get help?" Each time I thought about it, I flipped over, fluffed my pillow, and hoped that I could sleep. I tossed and turned all night long. I felt disgusting and ashamed.

My mom woke us up as normal for school the next morning. She had no idea what had happened, and there was no way I was telling her. It had already been a struggle for me to go to school, but now, I really didn't want to go. I felt dirty, disgusting, and ashamed. And I knew everyone at school would think so, too.

"Mom, I don't feel good. Can I please stay home from school?" I begged.

"Robert, get up and go to school. You'll feel better when you get there," she replied.

"No, I won't. Please, don't make me go," I pleaded.

Ben usually came to my mother's aid. He would encourage me to go and get me up and moving. But today was different. He avoided me. It was as if he knew something had happened, and he didn't want to face me. He never asked me or my brother about it.

I somehow managed to convince myself to get up that morning, but I knew I wasn't going to school, no matter what my mother said or did. Instead, I took the twelve-mile bus ride to school and walked home.

Eventually, I found some friends as troubled as me. We drank alcohol and smoked pot to escape our own personal pain. Soon after, my house became the party house. Ben hated my friends, so he left when they were there. But the pedophile never showed up when my friends were around which made me feel safe. The eerie part about the pedophile was that he always knew when I was home alone, when it was just me and my younger brother. Like clockwork, when we were home alone, he showed up. I got so numb to the sexual abuse that I taught myself not to feel anything. I convinced myself that it was not happening. My new life became drinking alcohol and smoking pot with my friends, skipping school, and praying each day that the pedophile would leave me alone.

I now had a lunatic inside my head; it was an overpowering negative voice that kept telling me I was no good and a loser. Most days, I wanted to die. What kept me going was the love I had for my friends. I lost hope that things would go back to the way they used to be: my mom and dad together, playing sports, and me laughing with my siblings. Deep down, I hoped that one day somebody would hug me and tell me that everything was going to be okay, but that hope dissipated, too. Nobody stepped up to protect me. I developed survival skills and rebellious negative behavior. Hurt people hurt others, as they say. And that's exactly what I did. I put my family through a living hell.

Ben and I fought most of the time after that awful day. But we were kids. Neither one of us knew what to do. We certainly didn't possess the tools to work through the spider web of emotions mixed with the chaos of our lives. I wanted nothing to do with my family except for my younger brother. I wanted to protect him, like my own version of *The Catcher in the Rye*.

My friends became my new family. All I wanted to do was hang out with them, drink alcohol, smoke pot, and escape the pain of the abuse and abandonment. I self-destructed, and no one could stop it; no one understood it, least of all myself.

After school one day, all my friends came to my house. One of them, Jackson, said, "Come on, Rob. We are going to rob this house. The people are on vacation."

Jackson was the ringleader of our group. He was five years older than me and took me under his wing. He was fearless and fun. We laughed about everything.

"We'll wait until it gets dark. I'll pry open the door and grab their big glass fishbowl that is full of change and dollar bills. You guys take whatever you want."

We all agreed. I never thought of the consequences, like getting arrested or going to jail. In fact, my insides tingled with excitement. The thrill of it made my living nightmare go away.

That night, four of us left at nightfall.

When we met outside the house, Jackson said, "Remember, I'm grabbing the fishbowl with the money, and you guys take what you want, but be fast."

My adrenaline spiked. I could hear my heartbeat in my ears, and my palms were sweaty. I followed Jackson to the back door. He pried open the door, and we were in. Jackson went for the fishbowl, my friends grabbed whatever they could, and I stayed close to Jackson. We were in and out in less than five minutes. We got back to the big tree and counted the money. It was at least two hundred dollars.

Jackson cheered, "Let's throw a big party at Rob's house."

We all knew the party had to end before my mom got home at midnight, but Jackson did exactly what he said: he threw a party. He bought five cases of beer, a big bag of weed, a quart of Wild Turkey, and a carton of Marlboro cigarettes.

We put cases of beer in my kitchen, and we all sat around the kitchen table under the adjustable dome light.

Stephen pulled the light down closer and said, "I'll clean out all of the seeds and roll a bunch of joints."

Jackson replied, "Cool. Rob, get over here. We are going shot for shot with this Wild Turkey 101!" He slammed the bottle on the table and set up two small glasses.

After about the fourth one, I protested, "Jackson, I can't."

The kitchen started spinning, and I felt like I was going to throw up.

Jackson screamed at me, "Are you tough or not? Take another shot!"

He punched me in the arm, and I kept going until we hit at least ten. I was so drunk. Jackson's face turned red from laughing so hard. My eyes were watery, bloodshot, and looked like little slits because I could barely open them.

"I don't feel good. I gotta go lie down."

I stumbled into the living room and lay down on the couch. I must have passed out because, at about 11:45 p.m., Ben pushed me back and forth, saying, "Rob, come on. Get up. Mom's gonna be home soon."

He helped me up and put me to bed, hoping my mom wouldn't know. There were beer bottles everywhere with cigarette butts in them. The house reeked of alcohol and cigarette smoke. Ben did his best to clean it up.

My mom got home a little after midnight. I was still drunk, but not as drunk as I was earlier in the evening. I heard my mom clinking bottles together.

Mom yelled, "Ben, get down here!"

I listened as Ben slowly walked downstairs to talk with my mom.

"Can you explain all these beer bottles with cigarette butts in them?"

There were at least seven bottles lined up on the kitchen table.

My mom said, "I found these bottles everywhere. Behind the living room chair, behind the couch, and in the bathroom. And the house stinks of cigarette smoke. What the hell is going on?"

She was yelling by then, but Ben didn't want to tell on me.

Ben said, "Mom, I just got home. I don't know what happened."

I heard the squeaking of the stairs as my mom got closer and closer to my room. She stormed into my room and said, "Robert Heine, where did you get the beer and cigarettes?"

"Mom, I found them by the side of the road."

Mom snapped, "Robert, where did you get it?"

I repeated, "I found them by the side of the road."

I would not give up my friends. I loved them more than I did my own family. My mom left with an empty look on her face. She was losing the war.

My friendship with Jackson gave me the strength I needed to endure the craziness of my life. He paid attention to me and made me feel important. He was not the best influence, but he stood up to the bastard who had ripped my soul out.

One day, we were sitting at our favorite spot, a stone stairwell going down to a side street. The exact spot where, a few years prior, I had jumped off the stone wall and cut my leg. Jackson, as always, was loud and laughing. The rest of us were smoking pot and drinking wine. Jake, our friend who owned the small engine shop a few miles away, was talking to me. Jackson snuck up behind Jake, stuck a firecracker in his belt loop, and lit it. Jake knew something was wrong but didn't have time to react. His eyes popped wide open; he looked like he'd seen a ghost. Jake jumped all over the place like he had ants in his pants.

And then the firecracker exploded.

Jake finally knocked the exploded firecracker out of his pant loop. His face was red. It looked as if smoke would come out of his ears. He glared at Jackson and shouted, "What the hell is the matter with you? That could have burnt me!"

We all laughed so hard we cried. Moments like that kept me going. They helped me to ignore the pain of my life.

We were all still teasing Jake when Jackson got our attention and said, "Hey, look, it's Booty Bandit!"

Booty Bandit, as he was called by everyone, was the pedophile who was abusing me.

Jackson yelled, "Booty Bandit, Booty Bandit." We all cracked up laughing. Jackson yelled louder, "Booty bandit, booty bandit!"

"Booty Bandit" turned around on his puke green bicycle and rode toward us. His hair was still braided in rows, and his right pant leg was rolled up. I didn't think he was cool anymore. He rode up to us and hopped off his bike. Jackson took off running. The bastard chased after Jackson and tackled him on the side of the road. He started punching Jackson in the face. Jackson laughed hysterically and said, "Is that all you got? You hit like a girl."

I stood there in awe. I was deathly afraid of this guy, and I couldn't believe Jackson had no fear of him. My friends were still laughing. I drifted off into my own thoughts, wishing I could stand up to this guy and not be afraid. He let Jackson up, got back on his bike, and rode off. Jackson got up, brushed off the dirt and leaves, and walked back over to us. He pushed me and said, "He hits like a little girl."

We all laughed and laughed and laughed.

Jackson was my hero, but the problem with Jackson and my other friends was that their influence created a hell that my family and I had to live through. Too many times, my mom came home to find me either high or drunk, and the house littered with cigarette butts and empty beer bottles. My mom begged and pleaded with me to stop, but I always responded, "Shut up and leave me alone."

If my mom kept pressing me, I would run off to the little bridge behind our house. I would sit on the edge of that bridge, swinging my legs back and forth until I calmed down and decided it was time to go back home. My mom had lost complete control of me. If life pressed me too hard, I would tell it to shut up, too. And then I would try to escape in any way I could. It was my way of surviving hell.

My seventh-grade picture. So much sadness in my eyes.

CHAPTER FIVE

Glimmers of Hope

"No matter how dark the world can be,
there is always a glimmer of hope."

- Laura Shone

It was 1977. I was thirteen years old. I had failed the seventh grade. The night before my last day of school, I heard my mother on the phone, pleading with the school not to fail me, "Robert is a good student and a good boy; he's just going through a hard time," she lamented.

But to no avail. My mom hung up the phone and sat on the edge of her bed, sobbing uncontrollably. I listened from inside my room across the hall. I wanted to go in and hug her and tell her it was okay, but I couldn't bring myself to do it. I was filled with too much hate. Too much pain. Too much resentment.

The last day of school finally came to an end, and I was glad it was over. It was a hot summer day, no clouds at all, and the sky was perfectly blue, my favorite color. Ben wasn't on the afternoon bus. I walked down the driveway with

JoÚ. It hadn't rained in a while, so when we walked down the driveway, we kicked up dust clouds. JoÚ purposely kicked his feet, making bigger and bigger clouds. He looked over at me and asked, "Rob, where's Ben?"

I replied, "I'm not sure. He probably didn't have classes in the afternoon and came home early."

"Oh," he said. "I'm going over to Hanson's house after I drop my stuff in the house."

"Okay," I replied. "Remember, we are leaving for Texas tomorrow, so get home early. Mom wants us packed and ready to go."

He said okay and went off to Hanson's house, just down the road from our house. I went into the living room to lie on the couch. I put the TV on. All the windows were open, and there was a nice breeze blowing through the room. I felt relaxed and comfortable, and I was so glad school was over for the summer. Before I could even sink away and get lost in the TV show, I got that eerie feeling that someone was watching me. Sure enough, the pedophile was peeking through the window. He climbed through the window with an evil grin. I froze and couldn't believe it was happening again. *The day before I'm leaving for Texas, this guy shows up.* I balled up my fists, furious. I wanted to fight, but before I could decide my next move, he pulled out his knife, tapped a button, and the blade flew open. The sunlight hit it just right and made the shiny blade flicker. He held it to my throat and said, "I'll slit your throat if you even think about fighting me."

He did his thing, climbed out the window, and rode off on his puke-green ten-speed bike. It would be the last time I would see him and the last time I'd be sexually abused.

I can't even say I hated him. Hate was not enough. The only thing my instincts could do to save me was make me completely numb.

I sat on the couch with my head in my hands. I felt so disgusting and ashamed. I said to myself, "Why didn't you fight him? Why didn't you run for help? Why didn't you slam the window on him?" The mental attacks kept coming.

I jumped up off the couch and took off running. I ran out the back door, through our backyard, and followed the path all the way to Decker's Hill like I had done so many times before today. I sat on the edge of the bridge, swinging my legs back and forth. I balled up my fists and started punching at the air. I felt so much shame. I felt unlovable and dirty, almost perverted. I wanted to cry but had convinced myself soon after the abuse started that I would not let him, anybody, or anything make me cry ever again. I was so afraid and felt like I could never trust anyone. At that moment, I knew that I would never open my heart to anybody.

My mind kept racing. I thought, "I don't want to go home anymore. I hate that house and can't stand to even be inside it. I don't want to go to Texas." I felt powerless, defenseless, and alone. I knew that nobody would ever help me. I didn't want to be around people. I wanted to run as far as I could, right off the face of the earth. I wanted to run away from myself. I felt completely hopeless; there was no way this situation or I would get any better. I hated myself. I hated life. And to make matters worse, I had a lunatic living inside my head.

We left for Texas the next day. I'm not sure how I managed to wake up the next morning and face my life. I don't know how my mom managed to take off work for an entire summer, but she pulled it off. When Mom woke us up, her eyes sparkled, and her face relaxed—the way she used to be before my father left. I knew my mom was happy to be visiting her mom and dad.

The lunatic in my head was quiet for now. I wanted to explain to someone what had happened the day before and that, most of the time, I felt hopeless and helpless. I wanted to be free of the pain. But that never happened; I told no one. I convinced myself that the events of the day before and all the other times had never happened. I stuffed it deep down and kept it all to myself, bottled up, waiting to explode. I was, however, relieved that for the first time in over a year, I could wake up without the fear of being abused. It was a small glimmer of hope.

Ben didn't really want to go to Texas, either. He didn't want to miss work, and he wanted to hang out with his friends. He spent a lot of time in front of the mirror lately, making sure his hair was perfect. I think he had a girlfriend and didn't want to leave her behind. Out of all of us kids, JoÚ seemed to be the only one happy to be taking a trip.

It was probably the worst summer vacation of my entire life. I continued the war I had going on with my mother. It wasn't intentional. The truth was that the war was raging inside of me, and my mother was just in the way. I rebelled against her on anything and everything. I made her cry over and over, and I didn't care.

My grandfather intervened one time and said, "Rob, don't talk to your mother like that, and be nice to her!"

I responded, "I can talk to her any way I want!" and took off running.

Running away was my new strategy for dealing with my emotions. My grandfather jumped in his white Ford pickup truck and chased after me. That's how the entire summer went—raging war and running away with my grandfather on my tail. But I could not outrun the insanity in my head.

Whenever I stopped running, the self-disgust and shame were still there. They made me feel like a loser. I could not shake it. I wished I could have screamed out, "I'm broken! I need help!" But I couldn't. No one knew the depth of my pain, not even me. I needed someone to hug me, hold me, and tell me it was going to be okay. I needed someone to validate my abuse and have empathy. I needed love. But in my state of mind, I didn't recognize love even though it was there.

After a month-long vacation in Texas, we finally headed home. I was glad to be back in New York, but I hated our house. I never wanted to set foot in it ever again. It was a reminder of the inconceivable torture I had to endure. The Texas trip had been an emotional roller coaster for my mom and me, and now, we had two weeks before the next roller coaster ride of going back to school.

Life resumed as normal for my siblings. Ben was glad to be back to his job and his mirror. JoÚ settled in and got back in touch with his friends in no time, too. But for me, things were different. Jackson had been arrested for robbing a local store and was sentenced to a year in jail. His absence split up the crew. I saw some of them occasionally, but it was not the same. Without Jackson, I didn't have a strong connection to any of my friends. He was the glue that held us together. I drifted, looking for things to do, and hung out with whoever was around. I was alone.

My mom didn't have to go back to work right away. It was comforting to have her home. Mom was more relaxed when she didn't have to work, and she was available to help us with our needs.

One day, she called out, "Rob, can you grab the newspaper from the front door?"

Without saying a word, I retrieved the paper and handed it to her.

Mom exclaimed, "Wow. Look what's on the front page. A local pedophile has been arrested for molesting two boys at the YMCA. He is in jail pending a trial."

I didn't say anything, but the news released strong emotions. It was disturbing. I felt like I had to run and hide, but at the same time, I felt a glimmer of hope, a relief that he wouldn't show up at the house anymore.

Before I could even make sense of what was going on in my mind, my mom said, "I told that son of bitch when he tried to pull JoÚ's pants down to leave my kids alone. And if he didn't, I'd deal with him myself!" My mom had no idea what had happened to me.

I was stunned. I sat there at the kitchen table with an empty stare, looking out the window, but I didn't see anything. It felt like my insides had collapsed, and I could not breathe.

"Mom, I'm going up to my room," I said quietly.

"Are you okay?" she asked.

"Yeah, I just don't feel good. I'm gonna lay down." I walked out of the kitchen with my head down. I lay down on my bed, and the lunatic in my head showed up convincing me that I was a loser.

The abuse was over, but the tragedy of it continued. I

would never be the same. I didn't wake up excited about the day. I woke up with a formulated plan in my head on how to survive. Because of the toxic shame I possessed, I felt dirty and disgusting most of the time. I constructed a wall around my heart and would not let anyone in or near me. I kept everyone, including my family, at a distance, a far distance.

The week before summer ended, my older brother brought home a brand-new racing bicycle. The bicycle was black with silver lettering. All the components were silver and sparkled in the sunlight. It had these things on the pedals called toe clips. He could put his feet in them and pull up on a strap, preventing his feet from slipping out. The experience of watching him ride that beautiful bike down our driveway gave me a beacon of light that I desperately needed. At that moment, I knew cycling was for me. I got a tingling feeling in my stomach, like the feeling I used to get when I heard the humming of my mom's sewing machine or the squeaking of the clothesline pulleys. I got little goosebumps on my arms. For a split second, my feelings of shame and hopelessness vanished. It was surreal.

I woke up the next day with a purpose. I sat on my bed and thought about the times when I knew I'd be playing third base for the New York Yankees or as a fullback for the Dallas Cowboys. Now I had a new dream: getting a racing bicycle like my brother's. Having a dream felt comforting; I hadn't had one in a long time. My newfound dream did not heal my pain or make it go away, nor did it make the lunatic in my head disappear, but it did give me the ability to temporarily forget about the insanity of my life.

My brother and his best friend, Pat, rode their racing

bicycles everywhere. I wanted to join them on their daily bike rides more than anything else. One day, I told my brother, "If I had a bike like yours, I'd be able to keep up with both of you."

He cheered, "I hope you do. You can ride with us anytime."

It felt good to have a connection with my brother again. Even though our relationship had changed for the worse the day I refused to play his game of protection, I still looked up to him. He always did well in school and never gave my mom a hard time. He did his homework and got up to go to school each day. I wanted to be like him, but the lunatic in my head always forced me to self-destruct instead.

I kept pestering my brother and his friend about being able to ride a bike with them. They were never discouraging because they knew I meant it. We came up with a plan.

"Rob, come on, we are going to the junkyard," Pat said to me. We walked to the junkyard about a mile away. I couldn't believe my eyes. It was breathtaking. There were old refrigerators, washing machines, furniture, car tires, and car parts, old bicycles, and bicycle parts. Anything people threw out was there, and the place was practically in my backyard. We searched through all the old bicycles. I managed to salvage an old ten-speed frame that was a little big for me but close enough that I could ride it. I found a front wheel, and then a little while later, a back wheel. We couldn't find a back brake, but we did find a front one. We didn't find all the parts required for a complete bicycle, but we found everything essential to make it possible for me to ride.

A friend had a can of gray spray paint at his house, so we spray-painted the bike gray and pieced together a rideable bicycle. I didn't have brake levers, so I simply pulled on the cable to engage the brake. I had the brake cable looped around the handlebar so it wouldn't fall. It also didn't have a front derailleur; derailleurs are the mechanisms that shift the gears. It had a rear derailleur but no cable, so the bike was stuck in one gear. However, I had one high gear and one low gear. To fix this dilemma, I would reach down and lift the chain from one ring to place it on the other. I mastered that tecÚique, which was quicker than using a front derailleur anyway. I got so good at it that I didn't see the point in getting a front derailleur. My wheels were not very true, but the bike worked, and I could go on rides with my brother and his best friend. Even though the bike was junk, I loved it. I built it and was proud of it. For the first time in a long time, I felt good. I could escape from the pain of my disordered life. Riding a bike was much faster than running.

Riding a bicycle prevented the small light of hope from burning out. My first serious ride with my brother and his best friend transformed me. It was a seven-mile loop with a screaming downhill. I was climbing the steepest part of the loop, not too far behind my brother and his friend. I couldn't keep up with them, but I could keep them in sight. I watched them climb and begin the descent. When I crested the climb, a feeling of ecstasy engulfed me. For a split second, time stood still. I forgot all about the chaos in my life. All the pain I felt inside vanished. I lost track of time and stress. Generating power to accelerate from one place to another without anyone's help was absolute freedom. I was free from the pain of my existence and never wanted to go home. I wanted to ride to eternity.

CHAPTER SIX

The Last Straw

"You could say that all of life is a series of last chances."

- Cythnia Voigt

In the perfect story, I would have built my junkyard bike, entered my first bicycle race, and taken first place. After the win, people would have surrounded me, clapping and cheering, and asking me questions. Fuji Bicycles would have offered me sponsorship to race for them. They would give me a bike just like my brother's, only in my favorite colors, blue and gold. But this is not the perfect story, not even close.

My newfound love for riding my bicycle became a great antidote for emotional pain and trauma, but it did not cure my compulsion for self-destruction. I rode that junkyard bike as much as I could, but I still had to attend school and participate in my life. My decision-making was warped. I stopped thinking about the abuse. I had tucked it away deep down inside of me, convinced that I would take it to my grave without ever telling anyone. But unfortunately, I still suffered its effects. The lunatic who lived in my head was getting stronger. The immense shame and humiliation of feeling dirty, disgusting, and unlovable were alive and well. I was an emotional trainwreck looking for a place to crash.

A few weeks after we returned from Texas, my mom decided we needed to find a cheaper place to live. A friend recommended a yellow duplex on the other side of town. It was much smaller but nice. I missed all the yard space we had at the old house, but I sure didn't miss the house. The old house was a reminder of the nightmare I had lived through. The move suited all of us. It was a needed change.

In 1976, I failed the seventh grade but passed the second time around. I limped through the eighth grade, and in 1979, I was halfway through the ninth grade, failing miserably. I rarely saw my older brother, although we still went for bike rides when possible. By then, my mom had no control over me at all. I had found new friends and was drinking alcohol and using drugs daily. If my mom took any of my drugs and paraphernalia, I would take them back and run away. If she had any alcohol in the house, I would drink it and tell her that I dropped the bottle, and it broke. It was slowly destroying my mom. She had lost hope in her situation and in me. I heard her pleading with my dad on the phone, saying she could not take care of me anymore. She was on the verge of a mental and physical breakdown, and I was completely responsible.

In late winter of 1980, I met up with my two friends, Kyle and Tony, in town. Tony lit up a joint, took a puff, and handed it to me. The three of us passed it around until it was gone. Kyle exhaled, moved closer to me, and whispered in my ear, "Rob, I have a plan. Let's rob this drug dealer I know tomorrow night."

Kyle stood about six feet one inch tall and weighed over two hundred pounds. He had a mustache and was only sixteen years old. I had known him for a couple of years. He lived up the road from my old house.

I jumped back and looked Kyle in the eye with a quizzical expression. "Are you serious?"

He laughed and looked at me without breaking eye contact, "Of course, I'm serious. The guy shoots pool at the local bar on Fridays. I'll go into the bar and tell him I want to buy a bag of weed, and when he comes out, we'll knock him down and take his supply."

"Wow, you make it sound so easy. What if he fights back or has a gun?" I asked.

Kyle brushed off my concerns with an unbothered air. "Don't worry about it. There are three of us."

I looked over at Tony and shrugged my shoulders. "I'm down if you are."

Tony and I had known each other for a long time but only had become friends recently. He was athletic and excelled in any sport he played. We had even played on the same Little League baseball team.

Tony nodded. "I agree with Kyle. There are three of us; we can handle him. I'm down with it."

We agreed to meet in town at 7 p.m. the next night, Friday. I hadn't yet learned that first thoughts are usually the wrong thoughts that result in severe consequences. I walked home that night, blowing smoke clouds in the air and thinking about the possibilities of the next night. Being able to blow smoke clouds was one of the only things I liked about winter. As I blew a smoke cloud, Jackson popped into my mind. I remembered the excitement and thrill of robbing a house with him. I missed Jackson. He made everything fun. I didn't get the same excitement this time. Robbing a drug dealer scared me. Jackson was not there to assure me that everything would be okay.

I started to think about the consequences. *What if this guy has a gun? What if he has friends looking out for him? Or even worse, what if the cops come and we get arrested for assault and drug possession*? I had never really thought about the repercussions of my actions before this night. But this time, I knew what I was about to do was a little more serious.

Despite this, I woke up the next morning convinced that robbing this drug dealer would be okay. Jackson would have punched me in the arm and said, "Don't worry about it. It'll be fine. You gotta be tough!"

We all met in town as planned. We stood in front of the Post Office, talking. The February air robbed us of warmth. We bounced on our toes, trying to stay warm.

"Here's the plan," Kyle asserted. "I have ten dollars. I'll go into the bar and tell the drug dealer I want to buy a dime bag. When he comes out to make the sale, we jump him."

We all agreed and gave each other fist bumps to psych each other up. My heart started to race, and I could hear my pulse inside my ears. The adrenaline gave me a sense of power. It was almost better than getting high. I imagined that's what made soldiers go into battle and overcome their fear.

We all walked over to the bar together, and Kyle walked in with no trepidation. The drinking age was eighteen back then, which he wasn't yet, but he could easily pass for it.

Tony and I waited outside, listening to the country music song playing on the jukebox. We both loved watching the bar scene.

I whispered to Tony, "Be alert. When they come out, we jump the drug dealer."

Tony didn't say anything, but he gave me a thumbs up. I peeked through the window, looking for Kyle. I didn't see him, but I did see the red lights flashing around the jukebox. An older guy was leaning on it, trying to decide which song to pick next. Then, I saw Kyle walking toward the exit. He was walking with a guy who was about five feet five inches tall. He had a red beard and mustache. He did not look intimidating and did not resemble my idea of a drug dealer. I had envisioned a big, muscular guy with tattoos and earrings.

As they left the bar, Kyle motioned for us to stay put. They walked over to the dealer's Jeep. We watched them make an exchange, and the dealer went back into the bar.

Tony and I walked over to Kyle. With confused looks on our faces, we both asked, "What happened?"

Kyle replied, "I changed the plan."

He walked over to the bar, peeked inside the window, and with a calm voice, he directed, "Okay, follow me."

He led us to the dealer's Jeep. Putting his hand inside his jacket sleeve, he punched out the passenger window. Under the seat, we found three big brown paper bags. We each grabbed a bag and ran as fast as we could down the old railroad tracks.

We made it to our hangout spot, a few railroad ties set up in a horseshoe with a fire pit in the middle. We sat on one of the ties, trying to catch our breath. What an adrenaline rush! My heart was pounding in my ears. I was exhilarated. Kyle lit a cigarette.

"Bro, we can hardly breathe, and you're lighting up a cigarette," I blurted out.

"We need to be able to see what's in the bags!" he argued.

"Yeah, you're right. But dude, I can't even think about taking a puff of a cigarette right now."

We used the glow of the cigarette and matches to see what was in the three bags. One bag had a bunch of rolled-up baggies with weed in each of them, probably dime bags. Another bag had a big plastic bag filled to the top with weed. The last bag had two plastic bags of pills, black beauties, and Quaaludes. There was more weed and pills in those bags than I had ever seen in my life.

Tony looked at me and then looked at Kyle. "Let's divide this up three ways," he declared.

I nodded in agreement, "That makes sense."

Kyle demanded, "We swear an oath of silence. No one tells anyone what we did!"

We all agreed. We each took a third of our score. I went home, took down an old board game from my closet, and hid all the drugs inside of it, hoping my mother would not find it.

I went to school on Monday with the intention of selling my new supply. Selling joints was easy, but getting rid of the barbiturates was a different story. Most kids I knew smoked but didn't use pills. By the end of the day, the entire school knew I had a supply. By Thursday, I was almost out of weed. I didn't want to sell all of it. I wanted some for myself. So I concentrated on selling the pills.

On Friday, my friend Ted saw me in the hallway and

whispered, "I've been looking all over the school for you. I know somebody who wants to buy some of your Quaaludes."

"Cool," I whispered back. "Tell him to meet over by the gymnasium after the next class."

I met the kid over by the gymnasium. He approached me nervously and muttered, "Are you Rob?"

"Yeah," I replied. "What's up?"

He whispered again, "Do you have Quaaludes for sale?"

"Yeah, I'll give you five for ten dollars."

He agreed.

I added, "Let's walk down by that classroom and make the exchange."

We ducked behind the lockers and made the exchange quickly. The kid went one way, and I went the other.

Out of nowhere, a teacher I didn't recognize grabbed me and slammed me against the lockers. He glared at me fiercely.

"I saw that. You were selling drugs!"

I yanked away from him and whispered under my breath, "You're an asshole."

"What did you say?" the teacher demanded.

I angrily snapped back at him, "You're an asshole. I don't know what you're talking about!"

He threw up his hands, shaking his head in disbelief, "I saw you hand that kid drugs!" Then, he grabbed my arm and marched me down to the office.

I don't know why I didn't shake loose and take off running, but I didn't. I wasn't worried, because I had nothing left in my possession. The teacher told the principal exactly what he saw, but the principal searched me and didn't find any drugs on me.

Unsuccessful, the principal sat behind his desk with a stern look on his face. "Robert, I didn't find any drugs on you, but I'm positive that the teacher is not lying. I have your file in front of me. You've already been suspended five times this year for multiple offenses, and you are failing all your classes. I have no other option than to expel you from school."

It was the middle of February, so I would miss at least four months of school, and, without question, I would fail the ninth grade. Inside, I was relieved—no more school. But then the principal called my mother. I could hear her crying on the other end of the phone.

The principal interjected, "I'm sorry, Mrs. Woods. I have no other option but to expel Robert. I'm going to need you to come to school and sign him out."

I waited in silence until my mom walked into the office with a weird look on her face. It wasn't the look that meant I was in big trouble. It was a look that indicated defeat. Her eyes were red, and her face was puffy. She had just finished crying.

My mom approached where I was sitting in the waiting area outside the principal's office, a familiar spot for me. She looked at me in disgust, "Robert, what am I going to do with you?"

I had no response.

The principal heard my mom's voice and stepped into the doorway of his office, calling, "Mrs. Woods, please come in."

They spoke in private for about five minutes. My mom came out of the office with tears in her eyes. She sniffled. "Come on. Let's go."

My mom didn't say a word all the way home. It was twenty-five minutes of silence. My mom stared straight ahead all the way home. She never once looked over at me.

When we entered our house, in a lethargic voice, my mom said, "I'm not feeling well. I called in sick to work today. I'm going up to my bedroom to lie down."

I replied, "Okay."

My mom went upstairs, and I went to the kitchen to make a sandwich. I sat down with my sandwich and turned the television on. Then, I heard my mom vomiting upstairs. I ran upstairs to her room as fast as I could. My mom was laying on her bed holding a small garbage pail out to the side of the bed. I watched her sit up and begin throwing up a brown liquid into the pail. Her face was devoid of color, and she looked panicked.

She shrieked, "Rob, call this number and ask for Barbara! When she gets on the phone, tell her you're Lola's son and that your mom is throwing up blood."

"Are you sure it's blood?" I questioned.

"Yes!" my mom yelled. "Call Barbara immediately!"

That scared me. I wanted to run as far away from the situation as I could. But I couldn't. My mom needed me. Deep down, at least that regard for her life was able to slice through my hatred and ennui. I picked up the phone on her nightstand and called the number.

"Hi, can I speak with Barbara?"

"Hi, this is Barbara." I heard on the other end. I had met Barbara a few times before and recognized her voice. She was the Registered Nurse at my mom's workplace.

My voice quivered as I replied, "This is Lola's son, Rob.

My mom is throwing up blood. She told me to call you and that you would know what to do."

"Rob, tell your mom to lie in bed, elevate her feet above her head, and call an ambulance. Call me back after you call an ambulance!" she exclaimed.

"Okay," I fearfully replied. My whole body was trembling.

"Mom, we have to elevate your feet," I nervously mumbled.

I grabbed some pillows and blankets and stacked them as high as I could make them. I lifted my mom's legs and put them on the pile of pillows and blankets.

I grabbed the phone again to call the ambulance but dropped it. I picked it back up and made sure I had a dial tone. I wanted to cry but did not know how anymore. I dialed zero.

"Operator, can I help you?"

"My mom is really sick and needs an ambulance," I whimpered. I managed to give her the necessary information. Within minutes, I heard the sirens.

I called Barbara back. "The ambulance is on the way. I can hear the sirens."

"Rob, you did great!" Barbara assured me. "Tell your mom I'll meet her at the hospital."

CHAPTER SEVEN

Bicycle Racing

"I learned the solace of routine. I developed a way to ride the pain."

- Frank Shorter, 1974 Olympic Marathon Gold Medalist

I stood watching the ambulance drive off with my mom. I didn't know what to do. I felt scared and alone. I also felt guilty because I felt that my constant rebellious behavior was destroying my mom. On several occasions, my older brother and sister told me I was driving my mom to a nervous breakdown. I did not have the psychological tools to pause, self-reflect, and assess the direction of my life. I did not give thought to any of my poor decisions and the negative impacts they would have on those who loved me, particularly my mom. I wish I could have relied on God and had faith and hope that all would be well, but I had not learned about God yet. I had not learned about God's silver linings.

That day, my mom was diagnosed with bleeding ulcers.

Her stomach hemorrhaged. Had I not called my mom's friend and followed her instructions, my mom would have died. She had vomited a lot of blood. The doctors removed more than half of her stomach, and she needed a blood transfusion. She was hospitalized for two months.

My only option now was to move in with my dad. JoÚ stayed with a friend until mom got better, and Ben was old enough to stay home by himself. My sister had her own apartment.

My dad had moved into a fancy two-bedroom apartment with his new girlfriend, Loie, about thirty miles from my mom's. There were eight buildings in the apartment complex, four on one side of the street and four on the other. Like the Pete Seeger song, "Little boxes on the hillside, and they all look just the same," they were white with brown trim and fancy designs etched on each of the windows. The lawns were manicured to perfection. It was obvious that the complex was for professional working adults. To me, that was "rich people." I didn't know how to act.

I stepped into the apartment, and Loie greeted me with a big smile. "Hi. How are you? How was the drive over?"

I shrugged. "It was okay."

The inside of their apartment caught me off guard. It was neat and orderly. Not what I was used to. There was a huge couch and love seat to match. There were little ornaments on the matching coffee table and a set of coasters. A large color television sat on top of an entertainment center, and behind closed glass doors sat a high-end stereo system. The wall-to-wall carpet was light yellow and looked brand new. I had to take my shoes off at the front door.

Everything had a designated place. I felt uncomfortable,

as if I did not belong. I had stumbled into an unfamiliar, new world. Loie took my hand and showed me to my bedroom. It was set up charmingly, with a twin bed, a dresser, a nightstand, and a closet with lots of hangers. There was a working fish aquarium with goldfish against the wall opposite my bed. I could stare at it if I was lying in my bed.

She asked, "Do you like it?"

"Yeah, it's great," I told her.

I survived my first day with no issues. I lay in bed that night wondering why the lunatic that lived in my head had not shown up. Why wasn't he telling me the awful, rotten things about me, reminding me that I was a loser? I realized that the gremlin showed up when I experienced intense emotions—when I got really scared, felt insecure, confused, or mad as hell. And for some reason, not feeling any of those emotions, subconsciously, I think I needed a break from my old, exhausting life. A different direction was in order. My other life was one mess up after another making me numb. I didn't want to be there, but I knew I didn't have a choice, so I didn't think about it. I pushed it far away like everything else I didn't like.

My dad supervised a facility that housed juvenile delinquents, which was kind of ironic. Loie worked at IBM. They were gone all day, and I had the apartment to myself. I wouldn't be attending school for at least five months, so I assumed I could withdraw into my own little world of sleeping late, lounging around, and watching television.

However, my dad expressed his expectations for me and said, "While you are out of school, I want you to go downtown and look for a job."

I laughed when he told me that and said, "What kind of job?"

He responded, "Washing dishes at one of the restaurants."

I was not thrilled about the prospect of getting a job, and my dad could tell by the expression on my face and the way I shrugged my shoulders. I had a blank stare, like a deer who had just been blinded by the bright lights of a car.

He added, "Your brother told me how badly you wanted a racing bicycle. Find a job and save your money for the next few months, and you can buy one. I'll even chip in a little to help you." It was a good plan, on my dad's part, to begin mending our broken relationship. I felt a sense of gratitude. It felt like my dad cared. Reviving my dream of owning a new bicycle gave me renewed hope.

I could not stop thinking about the possibility of buying a brand-new racing bicycle. Four years prior, I had watched my brother ride his down our driveway. I remembered the goosebumps and how I knew that riding and racing a bicycle was meant for me. The following day, I ordered a Fuji Bicycle catalogue and checked the mailbox religiously for its arrival.

A few days after arriving at my dad's apartment, I ventured out the door in pursuit of my first job. The walk to the center of town took less than ten minutes. I arrived at the clock tower building, a red brick building that resembled a church. At the apex, just below the steeple, sat a large black clock. I sat on the top step of the unused building and watched the cars go by. Most of them were fancy, expensive cars.

The prospect of finding a new job felt exciting, but at the same time, I felt alone and missed my brothers and my mother. I wondered what they were doing and thought about how JoÚ and I used to share a room. I wished they were there with me. Sadness crept in and I wanted to cry. But I would not allow it. Tears were for sissies, I thought. And if I didn't shut down my sad feelings, the lunatic would come back.

Jumping to my feet, I tried to psych myself up. "I'm going to find a job!"

My first stop was the supermarket. I grabbed an application and told them I would bring it back the next day. I thought it was cool to have a grocery store within walking distance. At home with my mom, it took at least a twenty-minute drive by car to get groceries.

Down the street from the supermarket were the Five and Dime, the hardware store, the drug store, and the delicatessen. I stopped at each, but none were hiring. I did not get discouraged. Surprisingly, I felt a sense of pleasure traversing through town. I had a purpose. I thought to myself, "Living here might not be so bad after all."

As I reached the end of Main Street, I noticed a house a few blocks away that resembled a mansion. It looked like a place for the rich and famous. I walked up to the building and read the sign out front. It read, "Fine Dining, Golf, and Relaxation." Looking it over, I contemplated the possibility of working there. It was too extravagant for me, and I thought, "There's no way I'm going in there."

But before I could talk myself out of it and walk away, a man wearing a chef's hat saw me standing there and asked, "Can I help you?"

Stumbling for words, I managed to spew out a response, "Maybe. I'm looking for a job washing dishes."

He replied, "It's your lucky day. I need a dishwasher. Come back tomorrow around 9 a.m."

"I'll be there." Just like that, I landed my first job. I couldn't believe it. I felt elated, accomplished even. I couldn't wait to tell my dad.

But it was a dish washing and food prep job, and it sucked. The guy who offered me the job, Dick, turned out to be my boss. He mistreated me.

Once, when I was ladling butter onto lobster tails, he grabbed the ladle out of my hand and said, "What, are you dense? You swirl the butter in one quick motion," and angrily demonstrated how to do it. I had never even eaten lobster before, let alone prepared it. He expected me to know how to do things and became angry if I didn't. He was not a good teacher, and he was a terrible boss.

I wanted to take the ladle and smack him in the face with it. I just looked at him with disdain and did my best to cover the lobster tail evenly with butter.

Another time, I was rinsing pots with warm water. Dick grabbed the pot out of my hand and said, "You really are stupid. I told you over and over to rinse the pots and pans with cold water." But he had never instructed me to do that.

I regarded him with hatred. I could feel my ears getting red. I was furious and close to punching him in the face. But I didn't. I wanted that racing bike.

Payday was every Friday, and I would receive a brown envelope with my cash money in it, the amount written on the outside of the envelope. Dick tried to convince me and some other co-workers to play poker with him on paydays. But I knew better. I wanted to save my money.

The Fuji catalog arrived. I knew exactly which bike I

wanted and how much money I needed. The local bicycle shop had one in stock. It was about forty miles away. My plan was in place and supported by my dad. I wasn't going to let my boss swindle me out of my money or spoil my plan.

The big day arrived. I received the pay envelope that gave me enough money to purchase my new bicycle. I felt excited and scared at the same time. A paradox. I could not sleep that night. I lay in bed, thinking, "I haven't felt this excited about life in a long time." It reminded me of my younger years before "the grenade" exploded in my house. It felt good to feel good again. I wanted it to stay.

It was a warm sunny summer day. My dad drove me to the bike shop so I could get my new bike. I had a lot of trepidation and constant attacks from the lunatic in my head. It said things like, "The bike you get will probably be damaged. They're not going to have the one you want. You don't deserve a new bike."

My dad noticed the eerie silence in the car. He looked over at me and said, "Son, we're almost there."

It was good timing because it stopped the lunatic's momentum. My response was simple: "Yup, can't wait to get there."

We arrived at the shop with no problems; everything went smoothly. The bike was not damaged, they had the model in the blue and gold colors I wanted, and I had enough money. I didn't end up needing my dad to help pay. The bike was fully mine. I earned it. With the little money I had left over, I purchased a copy of the magazine *Bicycling* and the latest edition of *Velo News*, a cycling newspaper. The shop assistant helped us put the bike in the back seat and showed me how to use the quick-release mechanisms to remove both wheels.

Halfway home, my dad pulled over and said, "Do you want to ride the rest of the way home?"

I looked over at him with a huge smile on my face and goosebumps on my arms, "Yes, I do. Thanks, Dad."

I rode home on my new racing bicycle, floating on a cloud. I loved it. The bike rode so smoothly. I had to get used to using brake levers and shifters because my last bike didn't have any. The ride home inspired me to want to race bicycles professionally. I wished I could have shared the moment with my brother Ben and his friend Pat, but it didn't matter. I had my new bike, and I felt happy.

I read the *Bicycling* and *Velo News* cover to cover. I learned about Greg Lemond, the United States junior national road cycling champion. My childhood idols were Bobby Murcer and Robert Newhouse. I now had a new idol. Even though my dad once said, "Robert, your idols have clay feet. Don't put too much faith in them," it didn't stop me from idolizing Greg Lemond. I read everything I could find about him and wanted to follow in his footsteps. Greg was becoming like a god to me. When I found out Greg and I practically shared the same birthday, I knew it was my destiny to become a cycling champion like him. It was a good omen, I thought.

My dad allowed me to keep my bike in my room. I picked out the perfect spot and constantly stared at it. I inspected it for dirt regularly and kept a cleaning rag nearby to keep it shiny. A few days after purchasing it, I decided I was going to take a risk and ride the thirty miles to my hometown to ride with Ben and his racing friends. I knew most of the back roads and had mapped out my route. The night before my adventure, I lay in bed thinking about it. *What if I get hit by a car, turn onto a road that does not have enough shoulder, or get lost? What about all the country homes that have big dogs that could chase me?* I kept thinking about how things could go wrong. However, strangely enough, I also thought about how exciting it would be to pedal myself all the way back home. I thought about the freedom it would give me. My determination to make the trip quieted the lunatic in my head.

I waited for my dad and Loie to go to work before I took off on my long ride. I did not tell them because they would say no. I figured it was easier to ask for forgiveness than to ask for permission.

As a novice cyclist, I had no knowledge of bicycle repair. In the case of a flat, I did not have a spare tube or pump. I knew nothing about hydration and fuel, and I only had a few dollars in my pocket. In practical terms, I was unprepared to make the long trip there and back. But it did not stop me. I rode off with determination and the thrill of a new adventure.

Just four miles into my ride, I looked ahead and saw a long climb, the highest ascent I had ever encountered. I could see the road, the twists and turns, and the steady inclines. It looked like the road would never end. My first instinct was to stop, turn around, and go home. Instead, I told myself that if it got too steep to pedal, I would just get off and walk. To my surprise, I was able to climb that hill with relative ease and any other hill along the way. Each successful climb built my confidence. I felt accomplished and proud. I no longer felt like a degenerate who always messed up. On my bike, I could accomplish anything.

Climbing steep hills and mountains gave me a sense of self-worth, something I hadn't felt in a long time. I could now go anywhere I wanted on my own. It opened a new world for me. I arrived at Ben's friend's house in less than two hours. Ben and his friends inspected my bike and gave me lots of compliments and high-fives for completing the journey. I was grinning from ear to ear.

Ben's friend asked, "You rode thirty miles to get here?"

"Yeah, I will ride thirty miles to get home, too."

Ben looked over at me approvingly, "I'm proud of you, brother. You finally got your own bike." After a moment, he added, "We are starting up a racing club. Our races will be on Saturday afternoons. Make sure you're here."

I replied without hesitation, "I'll be here!"

I made it back home that day with tired legs. My quads and calves let me know they were there every time I got up to walk. They were tight and ached as if somebody had used them as a punching bag. But there was something magical about tired legs, a tired mind, and a tired body. I liked it, and I wanted more. It not only made me feel accomplished but complete as well. I understood what Frank Shorter meant when he said, "I found a way to ride the pain." I had a lot of pain to ride away from.

The long ride to my hometown turned out to be much more than a long bike ride. It gave me freedom—freedom to explore and freedom to be myself. It gave me a sense of dignity. On a conscious level, I was no longer suffering from trauma and abuse; I had convinced myself that everything with me was good. On a subconscious level, I knew there was a constant internal struggle. Impending doom was always lurking. While the possibility of racing in my hometown was exciting, it was a constant mental battle to stay positive.

I could not contain my excitement though, as I made the trek to my hometown for my first bike race. Not thinking about the necessity of conserving my energy for the competition, I rode as fast as I could. I arrived a few hours before the start, full of adrenaline and excitement.

My friend Denis parked his tan VW Dasher about a hundred yards ahead of us. He was the official pace car. I was not prepared for the sound of twenty cyclists cruising all around me at twenty-five miles an hour. It was music to my ears. It sounded like a calm swarm of bees. It gave me goosebumps. Settling into the middle of the group called the peloton, I let them pull me along in their wakes. It was amazing. I didn't have to work hard at all. It was so much better than trudging solo for miles.

The course was a seven-mile loop, the same loop where I first rode my junkyard bike. The starting line, which was also the finish line, was about a mile from my old house in town, and it was marked by a bright green mailbox. The race was three laps, twenty-one miles. We talked and poked fun at each other for the first two laps, but things heated up as we turned into the third. The pace increased, and my breathing and heart rate did, too. Everyone began to get serious. My legs were a little heavy from the morning ride I took to get there, but there was no way I was getting dropped. I attacked on a slow but steady climb about three miles before the finish. I anticipated everyone countering the attack, but when I looked back, no one was there. I still had a lot of gas in my legs and thought, "Wow, that was too easy." So, I attacked again, and rode solo all the way to my first win. Beginner's luck? Who knows.

Our bicycle club took root and began to grow. Each week, new cyclists would show up. It was an exciting time. I didn't win every race, but I won quite a few and was always hunting for a victory. The muscles in my legs got so big that my brother and his friends said, "Rob, you need to see a doctor. There is something wrong with your legs."

That was negative food for the lunatic. It gobbled it up and said, "Yeah, Rob, you have deformities in your legs. Your idea of becoming a professional cyclist is stupid!"

I did see a doctor, and he said, "Robert, tell your brother and his friends there is nothing wrong with you. Tell them that they have never seen such well-developed quad muscles." I smiled, feeling vindicated. The lunatic shut up for a while. It was nice to feel good about myself.

I knew that cycling was prominent in Europe and often thought that if I was serious about my dream of becoming a professional cyclist, I should find a way to move there. I had read an article in *Bicycling Magazine* on Francesco Moser, an Italian professional superstar cyclist. He said American amateur cyclists put more work in during their training than professional cyclists. He said, "The pros don't so much train for racing as they race for training. The long, hard rides that prepare them for the spring classics and summer's major tours come in the year's first events, not in training sessions." Moser suggested that amateur cyclists in America should spin and ride smaller gears for the first thousand miles of the cycling season. I knew I wasn't going to Europe anytime soon, so I followed this suggestion.

Entering the early spring of 1982, I was eighteen. I learned a lot about training, racing, and some basic bicycle mechanical maintenance. For early spring training, I followed Moser's suggestion but took it to the next level. A friend built me a fixed-gear bike, which I still have in my possession. A fixed-gear bike has one gear, and the rider cannot coast. The back wheel and the pedals spin together. When the rider pedals, he/she drives the wheel. But going downhill, it's the opposite. The wheel drives the cranks/pedals.

My friend told me, "Rob, ride the fixed-gear bike before the racing season. You will develop the perfect pedal stroke."

A perfect pedal stroke is an efficient and powerful motion that maximizes energy output while minimizing stress on the body. The riders learn to use their quad muscles to slow down the bike. Initially, I was afraid of that bike. The first time I rode it, I stopped pedaling for a second, and it almost threw me off. But I overcame that fear and kept riding it. I learned to use my quads to slow the bike down and developed a great spin. I rode that fixed-gear bike for a thousand miles before I got back on my road bike. When I did, my pedal stroke was silky smooth. I no longer bounced up and down, and I was able to keep my cadence above ninety RPMs. With high revolutions for speed and climbing steep grades, I now performed like a sports car.

At one of the early club races that year, two Italian cyclists showed up at the start line. They were from New York City. The other club riders and I looked around at each other, wondering, "Who are these guys?" They both rode beautiful Guerciotti bicycles and were suited like professionals. Most of us rode in cutoff jeans and T-shirts.

Normally, the race director, who generally rides in the pace car, waves a green flag to indicate the start of the race. We considered Denis to be our race director. He started every race by slowly taking off in his tan VW Dasher.

The race had a rolling start. A rolling start is when all the riders ride slowly together following the pace car until the car pulls away and the racing begins. There was a lot of chatting and poking fun at each other, but no words were exchanged with the two new guys. They went right to the front of the peloton and set a fast pace. I settled in the middle. The race still consisted of three seven-mile laps, twenty-one miles total. We got to the climb on the back side of the course, and the two Italian cyclists accelerated, as if they had been shot out of a cannon. None of us could handle the attack. I went after them with all the power I had inside of me. I got close to them, but no one else was with me. I kept them within my eyesight for the entire race. But each time I got close, they would pick up the pace. And that's how the race finished. The two Italians in first and second, and me in third.

After the race, the two Italians hung around. The older of the two, Al, handed me his business card. "We own a business not far from here," he told me. "Give me a call, kid. You have potential."

Later, I called him, and he took me under his wing.

I trained with Al a few times a week. During one of our rides each week, we would do interval training. We'd pick a telephone pole as a starting point and sprint for two more poles. We did that at least ten times.

On long rides with steep climbs, Al would say, "Don't be a hero and get to the top and stand there. Push harder over the top. It teaches your heart to recover faster." I looked up to Al and listened to everything he had to say. His brother, Tony, took me to some of the bigger races down in Long Island, NY. We raced our bikes with two hundred other riders around Nassau Coliseum. I gained a ton of experience in pursuit of my professional cycling future.

As my brother and his friends went off to college, our cycling club died out, and my quest for riding professionally faded. I stayed in contact with Al, but it was sporadic. He had business responsibilities taking up most of his time, and his brother Tony moved back to NYC. I had life responsibilities that required my attention too, and my desire to become a professional cyclist would not meet that demand. With the loss of cycling connections, I found myself surrounded by negative influences again. It was like waking up from a dream that was too good to be true. I had held onto the dream of racing professionally, hoping that one day I would train with Greg Lemond. Instead of my cycling career blossoming like his, it began to dissolve. Greg was rising to international fame; I was bound for jail.

My first bicycle race. My brother's friend helped me put air in my tires.

CHAPTER EIGHT

Love, Marriage, and Addiction

"The most difficult times for many of us are the ones we give ourselves."

- PEMA CHODRON

LIFE AT MY dad's was consumed with riding my new bicycle. I also connected with some people in the neighborhood and developed a social network, all similar to the friends I had in my hometown—troublemakers and druggies. My best friend, Jiminy, was a lot like me; we were inseparable. The only difference between us was that I rode bicycles, and he didn't.

One night, when Jiminy could not find a ride home from his girlfriend's house in New Jersey, he stole a pink Cadillac to drive home. He stole that particular car because the keys were in it. On the way home, he was chased by the police and crashed the Cadillac right behind his house. We always teased him about it. Even people who didn't know him said, "Aren't you the guy who stole the pink Cadillac?" Jiminy taught me a lot about survival on the street; he also taught me how to sell weed and rob drug dealers. We did all kinds of insane stuff together.

It was early winter in 1980, during the Christmas holiday season. Jiminy and I were hanging out. We bought a bag of weed and rolled up several joints, which we sold to buy more, of course. It's called "flipping a bag." I learned that skill from Jiminy.

We were sitting there, rolling joints, when Jiminy said, "Racquel likes you."

"Who?"

He chuckled. "Earvin's sister, Racquel. She likes you."

Earvin and I played basketball at the local park. I knew Racquel was his sister because she would hang out with her friends at the park while we played ball. I never even considered asking her out. She was way too pretty to be with a guy like me, so I thought.

"Stop playing! How do you know?" I exclaimed, with a big smile on my face.

"She told me. She invited us to her Christmas Eve party tomorrow night."

I sat there in shock for a few minutes. I still thought he was joking, but he wasn't. His expression was totally serious.

Jiminy looked over at me and said, "Dude, are you okay?"

Confused, I said, "Yeah. I'm all right."

I left Jiminy's feeling excited but scared. When I got scared, the negative voice in my head (the lunatic) showed up. Like clockwork, the attacks came. It started with, "Why would she like you? You're a loser! You have a pug nose, curly hair, and you're not attractive to girls. What could she possibly see in you?" I tried to shake it loose, but it wouldn't go away. "You know Jiminy was just messing with you. He likes to play head games. Don't get your hopes up." I hated that negative voice. It took work to shut it up.

Racquel was attractive, with appealing dark eyes and stunning jet-black hair. Her smile made my insides tremble. I still couldn't believe a girl as pretty as her had a crush on me. I knew that when she found out the truth about me, she would have second thoughts. I didn't make mistakes; I was a mistake. I was unlovable, dirty, and disgusting. The lunatic drilled that into my head.

I finally met Racquel at her family's Christmas Eve party. Jiminy told her that we were going. I didn't smoke too much weed or drink too much alcohol because I was nervous about meeting her. I knew who she was, but I had never talked to her. I was still in shock that she liked me. Her mom didn't care if people smoked in the house, so I lit up a cigarette, trying to look cool and to help me relax. Inside, I was trembling. The cigarette calmed my insides and provided me with a physical distraction, like a fidget toy. Jiminy saw how nervous I looked and bumped into me on purpose. It brought me back to the moment.

Jiminy laughed. "What's up, lover boy?"

I laughed, too. "Stop playing. I'm nervous as hell."

"Lighten up, it's a party," he said. "Come on, let's go outside and smoke a joint."

I only took a few hits because sometimes when I smoked too much, it made me paranoid. And I didn't want that to happen. Not tonight.

When we returned to the house, Racquel's mom was freaking out. Someone had put a cigarette out on the turkey thawing out in the sink.

"If someone doesn't confess to it, you are all going home!" she demanded.

No one confessed. It was a great distraction for me, though. I didn't feel as nervous anymore. We all got to stay, but it changed the mood of the party for a few minutes.

Racquel and I exchanged glances with one another throughout the night. She would smile, and I would smile back. I did not pick up her signals for me to go over there and talk to her. I was a real novice with girls. I experienced sexual feelings and wondered about it, but I struggled with a lot of confusion. The abuse had messed up my entire sense of self, including my sexuality. I was attracted to pretty girls, but my low self-esteem and shame-based feelings made me scared. I found it almost impossible to talk to them. So, when Racquel expressed an interest in me, I did not know what to do.

Finally, she came over to me and said, "Are you just gonna stand over here by yourself all night? I've been waiting for you to talk to me."

I tried to give a relaxed laugh and look cool. But it didn't work. I muttered, "I get nervous at parties. I'm not comfortable around a lot of people."

"Yeah, me too," she said.

And that's all it took to start a conversation. It wasn't difficult. In fact, it was easy.

With a big smile on her face, she commented, "I see you all over town riding your bicycle. Is that why you have a nice butt?"

I turned red. "I love to ride my bike. I race with a club in my hometown."

We continued sharing little things about ourselves, and

I finally said, "It's getting close to midnight. I'm sorry I didn't talk to you a lot sooner. I have to go home."

Racquel offered to walk me home, and then she asked, "Did you know I watched you leave Jiminy's house a few times and followed you all the way to town?"

I laughed and said, "No, I did not know that."

We left her house together, and when we got to my front door, I said, "Now I have to walk you home."

We left my house and walked back to her house. When we got there, the game started over, and we trudged back again.

"Now I have to walk you home." She grinned with her eyes sparkling.

We did that circuit three times, laughing and talking the whole walk. Neither one of us wanted the night to end. At about 2:30 a.m., I finally broke the cycle and said, "I have to go in. I'm probably in trouble."

We looked at each other, leaned in, and kissed. It was a short kiss, but it was my first real kiss. I immediately got that tingling, champagne-like sensation. It was startling. It was as invigorating as riding my bike.

As soon as I walked in, my dad grabbed my arm and pulled me through the door. "You told me you would be home by midnight, and it's two thirty in the morning!"

I tried to explain, but he didn't listen. I went to bed mad at him for yelling at me. I mumbled some curse words under my breath and walked away.

I lay in bed that night thinking about my walks with Racquel. I closed my eyes and fell asleep thinking of her. *I can't wait to see her again.*

When I wasn't riding or racing my bicycle, I was with Racquel. We were inseparable.

Jiminy caught up with me one day and said, "I should never have told you about Racquel. I never see you anymore."

I laughed. "Yeah, I'm in love." Racquel was my first real girlfriend. For the first time in my life, I felt normal. I didn't feel disgusting and dirty inside.

My relationship with Racquel progressed, and my dad recognized it. He sat me down one day and said, "Rob, you and Racquel are spending a lot of time together. If the two of you are getting intimate, I hope you are using protection."

I didn't say a word about Racquel being pregnant that day. In fact, it would be months before I found the courage to have that conversation.

About a month after our "man-to-man" conversation, I decided I had had enough of living with my dad. We were constantly at odds with one another. And his daily drinking was a huge problem. I got tired of arguing with him. I packed up my stuff and left. I didn't say anything to my dad or Loie. I stayed at friends' houses until Racquel could convince her mom to let me move in with her. It took a few months, but eventually, her mom gave up the fight, and I moved in with them.

I wanted to get a job and prepare for fatherhood. However, at seventeen years old, I didn't know much about responsibility, let alone parental responsibility. I was a high school dropout with no skills. Although I always had a façade that I wasn't scared of anybody or anything, inside, I was shaking. Just thinking about becoming a dad made me tremble. I thought, "How can I become a dad? I don't have a job, I didn't graduate from school, and I can't even take care of myself." I wanted to run as fast as I could to the little bridge at Decker's Hill, but that was no longer an option.

My new escape route was my bicycle. It gave me the freedom to ride away from life's problems. But I kept learning, one experience at a time, that I could not ride away from myself. Everywhere I went, I was always right there.

One day, Racquel and I got into a big argument.

"I'm pregnant, and you don't have a job. I don't want to live with my mother. I want us to get an apartment!" Racquel pushed.

I couldn't argue with her. She was right. But I had my own wants and needs, too. I wanted to get a job, but I didn't want to let go of my dream of becoming a professional cyclist. I didn't have the communication skills to articulate my feelings and aspirations to her. I was toxic and didn't know it. I blamed everyone else, including her, for my poor decisions.

I yelled at her, "I don't care what you want. I don't want to get a job. I want to race my bike!" When I felt betrayed or hurt, I'd attack verbally and then retreat into isolation. I grabbed my bike, hopped on, and told Racquel I didn't want to argue anymore and took off. I shouted, "I'm going to my hometown. I'll be back later!"

I loved riding to my hometown. It was therapeutic for me. I could work out my problems during the ride, and I always felt better afterward. It took about an hour and a half to get there, almost as fast as a car. My legs didn't even get tired. I could have ridden three times that mileage. I hung out with my friends for several hours, smoked some weed, and tried to forget about the complexities of my life.

Finally, I couldn't avoid it anymore, and I told my friends, "Guys, I gotta go. I need at least two hours to get home before it gets dark."

I grabbed my bike and started walking to the road when I realized my back tire was flat. I went back to my friend's house. It took more than an hour to get it fixed. Now, getting caught in the dark was inevitable, and my bike had no reflectors or lights. It was a dangerous situation. I dismissed the feeling that told me not to go. The guilt I had for yelling at Racquel and storming off forced me to ignore my fear. By the time I was halfway home, it was pitch dark, and I was frightened. I could not see two feet in front of me, but the biggest challenge of my ride was still to come. I had to descend a two-mile hill, and I did not want to do it. That eerie feeling began to build in my stomach, and I panicked. I could feel my heartbeat in my ears. I started the descent anyway, and that's the last thing I remember.

I woke up with Racquel and her mother's boyfriend, Mike, standing over me. Mike was tough. I once saw him beat up a guy twice his size outside of a tavern. He did some prison time and knew how to hold his own. I'm glad we got along.

As I lay on the floor at a stranger's house, I heard Mike shout at someone I couldn't see, "What the hell is the matter with you? Call an ambulance! Can't you see he's in shock?"

I found out I had been hit by a car and that someone had picked me up and taken me to their house. How Racquel and Mike got there, I have no idea. I did not remember giving the stranger Racquel's phone number.

I arrived at the emergency room. Only this time, I did not see the familiar Dr. Beauboff. The EMTs rolled me in and transferred me to a bed. The attending physician shined a light in my eyes, checking my pupils. He felt my arms and legs, checking for broken bones. It turned out that nothing was broken, and all I needed were stitches in a few places.

While stitching me up, he asked, "How did you get such big muscles in your legs?"

I sort of grunted and said, "I ride bicycles."

After he finished stitching me up, he said, "I'll be right back." He gathered up most of his staff. They all came over to my bed. He pointed at me and said, "Look at the quadricep muscles in this guy's legs!"

The compliment was a good distraction and made me think of the time my brother Ben and his friend made fun of my huge thigh muscles.

At about the same time, Racquel and Mike came over and asked, "How are you?"

"I'm okay," I replied, then I looked at Racquel. "I'm sorry."

Fortunately, she smiled, kissed me, and said, "It's okay. I'm glad you're okay."

I left the hospital with plenty of road rash but no broken bones. I did have an imprint of the car's bumper on the back of my left calf, though. And it's still there to this day. I lost a shoe, but not my bike. Knowing how important it was to me, Racquel and Mike retrieved it and threw it in the trunk of Mike's car.

Racquel supported me back to health. After the accident, she was hopeful that I would find a job and let go of my cycling dream. I was scared about becoming a dad, but nothing could change it now. Racquel was six months pregnant. Instead of assuring her I would find a job, I convinced Racquel that I had a future in cycling. I told her I was winning club races, and I had met two Italian cyclists from New York City who were coaching me. I told her that Greg Lemond was my hero, and I wanted to race with him. I told her all about Greg finishing third at a stage race in Europe called Critérium du Dauphiné Libéré and that Greg signed a contract with a European Cycling Team. I knew it was possible for me to do the same thing; I wanted her to believe in me.

Racquel pretended to be excited about it, but I think the accident made her afraid. She also knew my dream was an extraordinary one. I told her once, "Greg suggested to American cyclists in a *Bicycling Magazine* article that if races are not available, they should do motor pacing." Motor pacing is when someone drives a car, and the cyclist rides behind it to get the drafting effect. I convinced Racquel to motor pace me in our little Dodge Dart. And she did. She did her best to support me and my cycling dream and not pressure me to get a job.

When Racquel wasn't pacing me in our Dodge Dart, my friend Denis stepped in with his tan VW Dasher. A few days after I had been hit by a car, I bumped into Denis in town and saw something hanging out of his shirt.

"Hey," I said. "Your tag is hanging out of your shirt."

He laughed and held up what I thought was his tag for me to see.

"Look, it's a Brown Scapular." He showed me the brown postage stamp sized felt piece attached to a thick brown string around his neck. "It protects me from evil." The felt piece had the image of the Blessed Mother with the words, "Whosever wears this cloth shall not suffer eternal fire."

My eyes opened wide. "I want one."

"Go ask my momma." In my childhood, I had spent a lot of time at Denis's house with him and his brothers, Pat and Tim. Their mom, Mrs. Leap, was an amazing human being. She was a second mother to me. Whenever I was at her house visiting, she would insist that I sit down and eat. She always reminded me of Mother Theresa, now known as Saint Theresa.

So, I approached his mother with a sheepish voice, "Mrs. Leap, Denis told me to ask you for a Brown Scapular."

She smiled and with great excitement said, "Oh, Robbie, sure! Let me go get you one." She came back a few minutes later and handed it to me. "This Scapular has been blessed by a priest. You come get another one when you need it."

I smiled and put on my Brown Scapular. From that day on, I have always worn one.

Despite Mrs. Leap's influence, my behavior didn't change. I came home from a ride one day and walked into Racquel's mother's house, which was still my home, too. Mike was sitting on the couch with his friend from prison, Jeff.

Jeff addressed me, "Are you Racquel's boyfriend?"

Jeff was tall and intimidating. He had tattoos on his neck, arms, and hands. He had the demeanor of a serious guy, someone you didn't want to mess with. I wasn't scared of him, but I did have some trepidation.

I reluctantly replied, "Yeah, I'm Racquel's boyfriend."

"You're the guy who rides his bicycle all over the place."

I nodded. "Yup, that's me."

"Sit down. I got a proposition for you," he said.

I sat down next to the coffee table. He handed me ten

small brown envelopes that had the words "Hardest Hard Harlem" stamped on them.

"Here's ten dime bags," he asserted. "Put your bike to use. Sell these for ten dollars each. I'll be back in a few days to collect my money."

I smiled, liking the idea. "Consider it done."

"Go grab one of those empty margarine containers with a lid and bring it here," he declared enthusiastically.

I handed the container to him.

He pulled out a big Ziploc bag full of weed, grabbed a handful of it, and put it in the container. "Let's see how you do."

Then, he handed the container back to me.

I was thrilled. I'd found a way to make money with my bicycle. When Racquel came home, I said, "Guess what?"

"What?" she asked.

"I found a way to make money with my bicycle. I'm going to sell drugs for Jeff."

Racquel was not thrilled about the idea, but she was not opposed to it either. She knew Jeff was a good friend of Mike's and a genuine dude. She knew he would not take advantage of me.

I left the small-time of "flipping bags" to work for a serious dealer. Everyone in town knew Jeff. Now I was "big time." My relationship with Jeff progressed from dime bags to quantity. He now asked me to deliver pounds of weed to different addresses. Of course, I would use my bicycle for transportation. It was the safest way.

The day after my "promotion," I rode my bike to Jeff's house. I knocked on the door and heard a dog barking.

Jeff opened the door a crack a said, "Hey, Rob. Hang

on a minute. Let me put the dog away." After a moment, he let me in, adding, "Don't worry, once he knows you, you have nothing to worry about." Then, he instructed me to sit down.

I sat in a chair opposite the couch and coffee table and waited. I looked around nervously and noticed Jeff letting the dog into the room. He told me, "Be still. I'm letting Sarge out."

The dog was a large, short-haired, brown and tan German Shepherd, a beautiful dog. I knew dogs could smell fear, and I had some. I tried to pretend I wasn't afraid, but I was. Sarge immediately ran up to me. He sniffed me up and down, and then Jeff gave the command, "Watch."

Sarge sat about ten feet from me and watched me the entire time.

I nervously mumbled, "Jeff, can you put him in the other room? He scares me."

Jeff replied, "Maybe next time."

Jeff sat opposite me on the couch. He put his .38 revolver on the coffee table; it looked like a gun from the gangster shows on TV.

He looked directly into my eyes with a calloused look and took a drag of his cigarette. "Rob, this is a serious racket you're getting into. Remember, you have no friends in this business. Trust no one. I don't trust you. How do I know you won't come back tomorrow and rob me?"

I just nodded in agreement, trying to act tough.

Jeff's dog, tattoos, and revolver had my attention. I knew he was the real deal. He continued, "Never sell product to anyone you don't know, and if you sell smaller amounts, have two people run for you. You never do the selling."

I sat attentively and listened.

"Do you hear what I'm saying?"

I nodded. "Yes, Jeff. I do. I will follow your advice."

He leaned in. "I'm only going to tell you this once. If you cross me, I'll put a bullet in your head."

"I won't cross you, and you can trust me," I proclaimed.

He handed me a package with an address and told me to deliver it when I left his house. I put the package in my backpack; I did not even ask what was in it. Instead, I said, "I'll deliver it as soon as I leave here."

He handed me two crisp one-hundred-dollar bills and said, "Don't fuck this up."

Our first son was born in October of 1982. Racquel and I got married a few months later, in January 1983. I had finally found a way to ride my bike and make money. I rode hundreds of miles a week and told myself, "Police don't pull over people riding bicycles." And I didn't get pulled over delivering drugs. Jeff taught me well, and I followed his advice. I made enough money for Racquel and me to get our own apartment. Unfortunately, I was spending more and more time away from my new family. Instead of becoming closer, we grew apart. And it was my fault.

I loved being a drug dealer and having a serious connection. It provided me with a sense of power. I forgot about my screwed-up past. It gave me confidence. What I didn't realize was that my demeanor was changing. I was beginning to behave like Jeff, hard-hearted with an "I don't give a damn attitude." My lifestyle did not complement being a family man. I ran from my responsibilities of being a husband and father, and I justified it by saying I had to make money.

Racquel and I began to argue frequently. One night, I came home, and she said, "You're never home, and when you are, you are high or drinking."

She wasn't exaggerating. I had been getting high daily, and now that I was dealing, my usage had increased.

"I don't care," I told her. "I'm only nineteen years old. I want to live the life."

"I want to live a normal life and raise a family," she countered. Deep down, I did too, but I did not know how to turn my life around.

Instead of arguing, I said, "I'm leaving."

I returned two days later. I continued that pattern of running away from my troubles.

On one of my days away from home, I went to visit the Leaps. Mrs. Leap answered the door. She was so happy to see me. She invited me in and asked with genuine curiosity, "Robbie, how are you?"

I mumbled, "I'm okay."

She put her arm around my shoulder lovingly. "Robbie, you know God loves you and so does our Blessed Mother. I pray for you every day."

I had no idea what she was talking about, but I nodded my head in agreement.

She continued, "I'm so glad to see you. You came at a great time. I have some great news."

I couldn't imagine what great news she would have for me. I had a hard time looking at anyone directly so I glanced over at her and then looked away before asking, "What great news?"

"I am going to Lourdes, France, on a pilgrimage next week. I will be visiting a Grotto site where our Blessed Mother appeared to Saint Bernadette."

I looked at her, puzzled. With little enthusiasm, I mumbled, "That's great."

I thought to myself, "If there is a God and a Mother of God, they are not interested in helping me."

She hugged my shoulder. "I'm gathering people's prayer requests and leaving them at the Grotto." I had no idea that on February 11, 1858, a fourteen-year-old girl called Bernadette Soubirous said she saw a vision of a lady while playing at the grotto with her siblings. Bernadette saw the apparition eighteen times. The lady introduced herself as the Immaculate Conception. The sanctuary of Lourdes is one of the most visited Catholic shrines in the world. "Here is a piece of paper. Write down a prayer, and I'll leave it there for you."

"Okay."

I sat down at her kitchen table and stared at the blank piece of paper. I had no idea what to write. I had never prayed a day in my life. I finally wrote, "God, please help me."

Mrs. Leap took that prayer to France and left it at the Grotto of Saint Bernadette.

Even with Mrs. Leap's support in prayer, my emotional intake valve was closed. The trauma of my past was tucked deep down inside. The self-hatred and low self-esteem were still there, but the "gangsta" lifestyle hid them nicely. On the outside, I looked like I had it all together. I had money, I had a beautiful wife and a son, and I was starting to collect material things. I bought a new racing bicycle with the accessories I needed to ride high mileage. I had cash in my pocket, and I believed people needed me. On the inside, though, I was empty. In an attempt to fill the void, I turned to all the wrong things: drugs, money, power, prestige, and material goods. I avoided the internal feelings at all costs. And it was taking its toll on my marriage.

Racquel was getting tired of my shenanigans, and honestly, so was I. I experienced blackouts whenever I consumed too much alcohol. On one occasion, during a blackout, I wound up in the county jail for dangerous behavior toward police officers and possession of marijuana. Not remembering the incident, I had to read the police report to find out what had happened.

On another occasion, during a Grateful Dead concert, I wound up in jail again in another blackout. When I appeared in front of the judge, the judge said with a stern voice, "Mr. Woods, do not stay for the next show. I want you out of town as soon as you leave my courtroom!"

"Yes, your honor. I'm going home."

The blackouts and negative episodes were becoming a regular occurrence. As much as I wanted to, I could not put on the brakes. I knew my life was spiraling out of control. Inside, I felt like a loser.

During another blackout, I attempted suicide for the first time. My sister told me later that I called her in the middle of the night and said, "I'm gonna kill myself." My sister, my mother, and stepdad looked for me in the middle of the night, with no luck. The only thing I remembered about that night was taking a bottle of pills and waking up in a snowbank, missing a shoe. I got up, went home, and never told anyone, jumping back into the insanity of my life.

My life was moving too fast. Jeff had disappeared. No one knew what happened to him. He was either dead or back in prison. Because I learned the trade well, Jeff's disappearance didn't matter. I had other connections.

My pattern of self-destruction continued to plague me. Instead of developing a loving relationship with my wife and son, I became chemically dependent on drugs and alcohol. In that chaos of addiction and the fast life, Racquel became pregnant again.

Our next son was born in May of 1984. Our relationship did not improve. We lived in a hotel, home to all the drug addicts in town. It was not a place for raising kids. It was an old building with a damp, moldy smell, and it reeked of cigarette smoke from the bar downstairs. At night, the jukebox blared, and there were drug addicts hanging out in the hallways. We shared a bathroom with the entire first floor. Most of the time, when one of us used the bathroom, there would be a set of "works" (a syringe for shooting heroin) on the floor. It was horrific and disgusting. It was a great spot to sell drugs (and I did), but it was a dire place to have small children. We were harassed by the never-ending sound of someone knocking on our door, looking for "more."

My new connections afforded me an entirely different scene. Instead of making deliveries on my bike, selling pills, magic mushrooms, weed, and acid, they showed me how to sell cocaine. I was given a small package that resembled a wrapper from a piece of chewing gum.

One guy said, "Rob, it's yours. On the house." I had

no idea what it was. He could tell. "It's cocaine," he added. "You'll love it."

He showed me how to chop up the white powder with a razor blade on a small mirror. He cut it into two neat lines and rolled up a ten-dollar bill. He held one of his nostrils shut with his finger and sniffed up a line into his nose using the bill and did the same thing in the other nostril. He spread out two more lines and said, "Your turn."

I followed his lead. It was extraordinary. It was the best high I had ever experienced. I felt euphoric, beyond description. I felt an immense sense of joy and confidence. It gave me an immeasurable amount of energy—and I wanted more.

He asked, "Well, what do you think?"

"I love it, and I want more."

"I can make that happen. And if you're interested, we can make a lot of money together!" he exclaimed.

It was the winter of 1986. Racquel was a few months pregnant again. We had recently learned she was carrying twins, and it showed. I came home one day, and she was upset.

"We have to get out of this place," she demanded. "It smells in here, and the landlord won't let us use the hotplate anymore. He said absolutely no cooking in the room."

I agreed. "I hate it here, too. I got an idea to get us out of here quick."

"What's your idea?" she asked.

I pulled out the wrapper with the cocaine and convinced her to try it. I was completely ignorant of the fact that cocaine was dangerous to my wife and the fetuses.

Racquel tried a little and complained, "Ew, I don't like

it. It tastes like poison." She spit it into the garbage can, looked over at me, and said, "What's the plan?"

I said, "I buy some pure cocaine, cut it up with inositol, and sell it for a profit. Inositol is a white powdery substance that resembles cocaine. It is considered a vitamin, but it's actually sugar. My friend said we can make four times the amount we pay for it." I convinced her that this guy knew what he was doing and would show me everything I needed to know to make money.

Racquel hesitated before finally agreeing. "Let's do it."

I bought an ounce of cocaine from my new connection. He lived on the third floor of the same hotel. We sat in his room and bolt-locked the door. He had a flip scale, wax paper envelopes, and several jars of inositol. The inositol increased the weight but cost only ten dollars a bottle.

"Pay attention. You have to make two batches. One for the rich white kids, and one for the junkies," he told me.

"I don't understand."

"The rich kids," he explained, sifting the cocaine and the inositol through a screen to mix them up, "won't know that we cut the cocaine, but the junkies will. We can only step on the junkie's batch with a small amount of cut."

He taught me all the tricks of the trade. We sat there and bagged cocaine for hours.

When we were done bagging and prepping, he beamed. "I saved this rock for us." It was a large chunk of uncut cocaine. He chopped it up with a razor blade and spread out two lines for himself and two lines for me. He went first, and then me.

After snorting my lines, I felt super confident and extreme pleasure. However, within minutes, I felt like my heart was going to jump out of my chest. I sat as still as I could in his reclining chair. Afraid to move, I just sat immobile in my chair, worrying that any movement would send me into cardiac arrest. I was paralyzed. After about an hour, my heart stopped racing, and I thought I'd be okay.

Looking over at my friend I cautioned, "Don't ever do that to me again," with a slight grin on my face. I left his room with two brown bags full of small cocaine packages, one for the rich kids and one for the junkies. I had enough cocaine in those bags to send me to prison for a long time if I got caught.

I made it back to our room and showed Racquel all the bags I had. I told her about the rich kids and the junkies. We were not prepared for what was coming. People who lived in the hotel wanted to buy cocaine. It sold quickly. I tried to implement what Jeff had taught me about having a runner and not selling to people I didn't know. I did not know that cocaine was a twenty-minute high and that people get extremely hooked on it and want more. Or that they would rob and steal to get their next bag. After a few days, customers started knocking on the door with radios, stereo equipment, food stamps—anything of value—asking for a bag of cocaine. My friend was right. There was money to be made. I quadrupled my money in less than a week.

It didn't take long for me to acquire enough money to move us out of the hotel. We rented an apartment above the pizzeria in town. It was a small one-bedroom apartment with a bathroom, a small kitchen, a living room, and a bedroom. It wasn't the best place, but it was an improvement over the hotel. Our apartment had the aroma of Italian food instead of mold, mildew, and cigarettes like the hotel. Just before closing, I would go down to the pizzeria, and the owner would give me all the food that was left over instead of throwing it out. We had a magnificent view of the town, and we were within walking distance of all the local stores. It was a great setup, but Racquel and I were miles apart. I knew nothing about intimacy and love or how to be a father and a husband. I avoided her attempts of trying to mold me into a family man. Instead, I stayed high daily.

I continued to make a lot of money. I bought modern furniture and new appliances and always had cash on hand. Financially, things were going well. Only now, without giving it much thought, my cocaine habit increased. I was using it daily, an expensive habit.

Cocaine is a powerful drug. It made me feel hyper-focused and confident. I relied on it and became addicted almost immediately. I was not the only game in town though, and when customers went elsewhere, I consumed more than I sold, which put me in debt and on unbelievably bad terms with the other drug dealers. That is not a position anyone wants to be in.

Racquel gave birth to our identical twins in June of 1986. Because they were born with full heads of hair, everyone said they looked like little Liberace. After their birth, I wanted to straighten myself out and do the right thing. I now had four beautiful sons and a wife who was trying to love me. I did my best to be a good father and husband, but my chemical dependency and lack of emotional development always got in the way. I continued to make bad decisions.

A few days after the birth of our twins, I went to visit the Leaps. My home away from home.

Again, Mrs. Leap answered the door, having just returned from Lourdes. And she brought me several gifts.

"Robbie, I have a Brown Scapular, a Rosary, and some books for you."

It felt awkward when people were nice to me. With a timid voice, I replied, "Thank you, Mrs. Leap. I appreciate the gifts."

"The books were written by St. Louis de Montfort," she explained. "Read them and follow the instructions on how to pray the Rosary. Remember, Our Blessed Mother loves you very much."

She spoke with great confidence. I really did appreciate her love and concern. But my social skills were feeble. All I could mutter was, "Thank you."

"Robbie, please pray the Rosary. Our Blessed Mother will come to your aid."

"I will," I assured her.

"Don't ever stop praying, and I will pray for you daily, too. It is our greatest weapon against the devil," she urged.

She did not know that I had never prayed. I looked at her and felt the need to cry. In a broken voice, I said, "I will read the books and pray the Rosary."

"Hey, Rob!" Pat came downstairs, ending the conversation. "Are you still racing your bike? And have you read the newspaper lately?"

I replied, "I ride all the time, but I haven't raced in a while. And no, I have not read the newspaper."

He handed me a copy of the day's paper. I looked at the back page—the sports section—and read, "Greg Lemond coming to Goshen, NY. He will compete in a race called Cititour." I still followed Greg and bicycle racing. I knew he had just won the Tour de France, the greatest, toughest, longest bicycle race in the world. Bicycle racing was always in my mind, but lately, it had been a very distant thought.

Still, I was excited.

Back at home, I sat in my bedroom and embraced my new Rosary. I opened the book by St. Louis de Montfort and followed his instructions. Feeling awkward and uncomfortable, I made a valiant effort. No bolt of lightning, no bright light. It was a one-shot deal. I attempted to pray the Rosary and read the literature, and then I put them in a drawer and forgot all about them.

Racquel came home shortly after I put my things away and said, "Rob, look what the church gave us!"

She was pushing a blue stroller that looked like a stretch limousine. It was a stroller designed for twins.

"That's awesome. I'm gonna call it the Cadillac." We both laughed. It was good to laugh. "I spoke to Pat today," I told her. "He said Greg Lemond is coming to Goshen to participate in a bicycle race called the Cititour."

Racquel stopped for a minute, paused, and said, "Isn't that the cyclist you told me about when we first met?"

"Yup, and he just won the Tour de France a few months ago."

I met Greg when he arrived in Goshen, NY on September 14, 1986. It was the most amazing day of my life. My childhood friend, McGuinness, and I went to the race together. We arrived at the start line a few hours early. I tried to spray paint "Bravo Lemond" on the pavement, but a police officer came over and said, "You are defacing public property."

In Europe, fans who attend the popular bicycle races paint

the names of their favorite cyclists on the road, especially the famous climbs of the Giro d'Italia, Tour de France, and Le Vuelta.

"I'm honoring Greg Lemond."

He replied stubbornly, "I don't know who you are honoring; you can't deface public property. If you try it again, I'll arrest you."

I tried again anyway, but he came back and shouted, "I told you I would arrest you. Move along!" Instead of giving him a hard time, I gave up. My enthusiasm for meeting Greg gave me the strength to let it go.

Cycling teams arrived a few at a time. And then, out of nowhere, Andy Hampsten, an American cyclist, and his team parked right behind McGuinness's car. They put all their cycling gear on his car as they prepared for the race. Then, another car parked in front of McGuinness's car.

I screamed at McGuinness, "Look who's in front of your car!"

"Robbie, that's Phil Anderson," he cried out excitedly. Phil Anderson was an Australian Superstar.

I went over to Phil's car. It was just him and a woman. "Hi, Phil. Can I help you out?" I asked.

"Sure," he said. He handed me his bike from the back of his car. "Can you hold my frame while I put the wheels on?"

It felt like I was in a dream. "Absolutely."

He thanked me, and I wished him good luck.

McGuinness and I were surrounded by professional cyclists. It was a dream come true. It made me want more, but my life choices and my low self-esteem would not allow it.

Someone shouted, "Greg is here!"

He was the last cyclist to arrive. He pulled up in his team car, and a crowd of people swarmed the vehicle.

I pushed my way through the crowd. McGuinness shouted, "Robbie, what are you doing?"

I didn't say anything. I just kept pushing my way through the crowd until I arrived at Greg's team car. I opened the door, and there Greg sat with a big smile on his face.

I heard his dad say, "Greg, come on, you have to get to the start line."

I helped Greg out of the car and couldn't believe it. I had been watching him on TV and reading about him for years, and now, here he was, in the flesh. It happened so fast. I don't think he even looked at me. I don't know what led me to push through the crowd and grab his arm to help him out of the car. To me, Greg was a god. And in that moment, I felt like a god, too.

Meeting Greg gave me a boost of inspiration. I attempted to make my way back to racing bicycles and leave the drug world behind. I re-watched the recorded cycling videos I had. They gave the audience an inside look at Greg Lemond and his training buddy, Steve Baur. I wanted to ride and train with them, but my drug habit was out of control. I couldn't stop. I was in way too deep, and I needed help.

Not too long after the Cititour bicycle race, something extraordinary happened. I came home at two o'clock in the morning. Trying not to disturb my sleeping wife and children, I entered my apartment quietly, like I did every night. In the middle of our living room sat a big white swivel lounge chair. I always sat in that chair. I would take my shoes off and relax for a few minutes before climbing into bed. This night, like every night, I went to sit down in the lounge chair, but in that chair sat a man resembling Jesus. His arms were open, reaching out to me as if to give me a hug. I stopped, put my hands up, and shook my head hard to make sure I wasn't hallucinating, and then looked back at the chair.

I wasn't hallucinating; Jesus was sitting in that chair. I didn't say a word. Instead, I darted out of the apartment and ran down the stairs. I pushed open the two big main entrance doors and ran as far as I could until I couldn't breathe. When I finally stopped, I had to bend over to catch my breath. As I stood up, I realized I was standing in front of a statue of the Blessed Mother in front of a Roman Catholic Church. I couldn't believe it; I ran from Jesus only to run into Mother Mary.

I put my face in my hands and began rubbing my eyes. I mumbled, "Jesus and Mary, what do you want from me?" But there was no audible answer.

I walked back home and quietly entered the apartment. No Jesus in the chair, and my wife and children were sound asleep. I never told a soul. Who would have believed me anyway? Instead, I continued with my tumultuous life.

I dismissed Jesus and Mary appearing to me. I had too much toxic shame, guilt, and hatred to allow anyone or anything to get close to me. If God existed, I was sure He didn't care about me.

Then, my whole world came crashing down. Unable to kick my drug use, my habit put me in debt with drug dealers. I stopped paying the bills. I felt paranoid and anxious most of the time. And to make matters worse, Racquel took the kids and moved back in with her mother. The drug dealers showed up at my house and took everything I owned. I lost it all. I lost my family, my bike, all my expensive televisions and stereos, my furniture, and everything else of value. Most importantly, I lost myself. I sat there in the empty apartment, thinking about the little bridge at Decker's Hill. But it was not that simple anymore. Life had shark-like teeth that dug in hard and wouldn't let go. I felt abandoned, alone, and helpless. I was completely hopeless. I wished I could die.

The little bridge I ran to in times of distress was at the base of Decker's Hill. The little bridge is no longer there. But it still lives inside of me.

CHAPTER NINE

Recovery

"Recovery is not simple abstinence. It's about healing the brain, remembering how to feel, learning how to make good decisions, becoming the kind of person who can engage in healthy relationships, cultivating the willingness to accept help from others, daring to be honest, and opening up to doing."

- Debra Jay, Addiction Specialist

A few months before I lost it all, I got a call from my stepmother, Loie. She and my dad had gotten married and bought a house not too far from my childhood town.

"Hi, Rob," she said. "I need you to come to the house. I have something to tell you."

I replied, "Okay, when?"

She said, "Tomorrow evening around six, your brothers and sister will be there, too."

"Okay. I'll be there."

I hung up the phone and didn't think much more about it. My biggest concern was my cocaine addiction, not beating it but feeding it. My drug addict behavior was affecting the people who loved me, and I didn't care. I didn't care what was happening with other people, not even my own family. My only interests were getting high and staying high.

The next day, my siblings and I sat at the table, looking at each other. No one knew what to say.

I broke the ice. "Anyone want a beer?"

My sister and I made eye contact for a second. She wore a look of bewilderment, and I couldn't tell if she was disgusted with me for getting a beer or nervous about the meeting with my stepmother. My brothers didn't seem to care one way or the other. Both of them said in unison, "No, thanks."

I grabbed a beer out of the refrigerator and sat back at the dining room table. I twisted the cap off, and it made my favorite sound, "psht." I took a long swig. We all sat there quietly, waiting for Loie.

Finally, we heard Loie come down the stairs. She came into the dining room with an envelope in hand. She sat down and said, "I have some news about your father. He asked me to read you all this letter."

Loie pulled the letter out of the envelope, unfolded it, and cleared her throat. She had a troubled look on her face. She hesitated, composing herself, and then began reading.

"Here goes," she said. "My dearest children, I came to the hardcore realization that I have a problem with alcohol. It is probably no surprise to all of you since you have witnessed my drinking on many occasions. I admitted myself to an alcohol rehabilitation center. I will be here for the next twenty-eight days. I love all of you very much. I am in rough shape and did not want y'all to see me this way, so I asked

Loie to read y'all this letter. I have no idea what will happen next. I just knew I could no longer continue to drink, and I could not stop on my own. I love all of you very much and look forward to talking with each of you when I am released from rehab. Love, Dad."

There was complete silence. No one said anything. Tears rolled down my sister's face. "I want to go visit him," she said.

"Your father is not in a good place. He doesn't want any of you to see him that way," Loie replied.

My sister continued to cry and repeated, "I want to go see him."

I looked at my brothers, who had perplexed expressions on their faces. They were not crying but were certainly in a state of confusion.

I picked up my beer and finished it off in one long gulp. I put it down on the table, wiped my mouth, and said, "I really don't care. I gotta go."

And I left.

I didn't know anything about alcoholism and addiction. I did not know that it was a family disease. And honestly, at that time in my life, I didn't care. I wanted to be high for the rest of my life. While experimenting with drugs and drinking, it never occurred to me that it could lead to a drug-addicted life.

The first time I drank, I was ten years old. My sister overheard me and my friend Stephen talking about meeting up with some of our friends to drink wine at the "Big Tree." The "Big Tree" was a spot across the street from my house where my friends and I always hung out. I told my mom I was going out to play with some of my friends.

My sister yelled, "Don't let him! He's gonna drink wine with his friends at the Big Tree!"

My mom said, "Robert Heine, don't you leave this house!"

I begged her and said that Mary Alice was lying. Mom would not budge.

Soon after, Stephen came to my front door and said, "Rob, are you coming out?"

"I can't. My sister told on me," I told him.

He handed me the bottle of wine in a brown bag and said, "Hurry up. Take a big swig."

I took the bottle and drank as much as I could. My sister saw me drink it and ran to tell my mother.

My mother came to me and said, "Robert, let me smell your breath."

She smelled my breath and said, "You did take a drink."

Then, my mother smacked me right in the mouth and told me to go to my room. I ran to my room as fast as I could. I was furious and resentful. My anger was directed at my sister for telling rather than at my mother for smacking me. Regardless, I didn't talk to either one of them for the rest of the day.

I was eleven years old when I first got high on marijuana. A friend of my sister's, Tom, had just returned from a vacation in California. I was walking to my Little League basketball game when I heard, "Rob, come here."

I looked over, and Tom was sitting against a big red barn along the walking path. I replied, "Tom, what are you doing over there?"

He laughed, "I'm just hanging out. Come here. I want to show you something."

I knew Tom. He could ride wheelies on his bicycle from my house all the way through town and keep on going. I asked, "What's up?"

He reached into his pocket and pulled out a bag of weed. "Look what I brought back from California. It's purple sinsemilla."

I had no idea what that meant, but I said, "Cool."

He said, "Come on. Smoke some with me."

"No way. I'm on my way to my basketball game," I replied.

"Cool! You'll play even better." Tom filled a little water bong with "weed" and instructed, "Inhale as much of it as you can."

I did exactly what he said. I inhaled as Tom lit the bowl and then coughed out the smoke. It made me choke. My face turned purple. Tom convinced me to take another hit, and I had the same reaction. I choked until I almost puked. I felt this weird sensation behind my eyes. My eyes got red and puffy. Tom looked at me and started laughing. He laughed so hard he had tears coming out of his eyes.

Suddenly, everything seemed different. I felt the need to laugh, and life didn't seem so bad anymore. I loved how it made me feel relaxed. Everything seemed funny.

"Tom, I gotta go. I'm gonna be late for my game."

He laughed and said, "Good luck. I keep the bong right here if you ever want to use it." He pointed to a hole in the barn.

Everything was cool until I walked into the gym. The bright lights in the gym blinded me. It took a few minutes for my eyes to adjust. Suddenly, I felt paranoid. I thought all the parents in the bleachers were staring at me. With a dazed look on my face, I stumbled over to my bench, where all my teammates were standing.

My coach asked, "Rob, are you alright?"

"No, coach. I don't feel well," I replied.

He said, "Sit on the bench until you feel better."

I sat there so high. It felt like everyone in the gym was staring at me. I wouldn't look up. I couldn't stand it. I had to get out of there. Finally, I walked over to my coach and said, "I really don't feel good. I have to go home."

He said, "Okay. I hope you feel better."

I couldn't get out of there fast enough. Instead of saying to myself, "You idiot, don't ever do that again," I thought, "I can't wait to smoke more." As much as I loved playing sports, the feeling of being high was better. That event was a foreshadowing of what drugs and alcohol would eventually do to my life.

Like my friend Barry always said, "I was always looking for more." I spent many years looking for more. It never occurred to me that drinking alcohol and smoking weed would lead me down a path of self-destruction. I thought drinking alcohol was cool. I watched my dad, my mom, and their friends make frozen daiquiris at parties and pyramids with their beer cans during sports games on television. It looked like so much fun to me. Everyone laughed and fooled around. It was perfectly normal to see my dad passed out in the living room the next day, out cold, lying next to his pyramid of beer cans, the game score written on a paper plate leaning up against the pyramid. My mom even took a picture of him once, and we all loved it. I couldn't wait to be able to drink and have fun, just like my dad.

Before I turned twelve years old, I smoked cigarettes

and weed and drank alcohol regularly. It seemed perfectly normal to me. All my friends, who were at least five years older than me, got high and drank too. Why shouldn't I? I didn't realize I was using substances to escape from the reality of my parents' divorce and to numb myself from the pain of my trauma and abuse. It was my goal to feel good, have fun, and be cool. And that's exactly what I did.

Smoking pot and doing stupid, crazy things became a way of life. I thought Jackson forcing me to do ten bong hits in a row was a huge accomplishment. I had no idea that consistent use would lead me to a chemical dependency. It was a relief not to feel shame, fear, anger, or anything else, really. I was glad to be having fun. Getting high and having fun for the next fourteen years of my life was my adopted attitude. I never once thought drugs and alcohol were a problem; I just rationalized my poor decisions by saying, "I have crap luck."

When I left my dad's house a few minutes after Loie read us that letter, I dove right back into my addiction lifestyle, smoking pot, drinking alcohol, and snorting cocaine. I didn't even think about my dad being in rehab.

When I got home, Racquel asked, "What did Loie say?"

"She read us a letter from my dad. He checked himself into an alcohol rehabilitation center. He'll be there for twenty-eight days."

Racquel looked at me with a quizzical look on her face and asked, "What did you say to them?"

I replied, "I finished my beer and told everyone that I really don't care."

Racquel walked away without a response. She always liked my dad and did not know how to respond. We never talked about it again because within a few weeks, she would move out. I sat there for a minute, a little disoriented. An eerie feeling came over me, an out-of-body experience. I thought, "I *do* care about my dad." I remembered when my dad was my anchor. I thought about how, when I was in the presence of my dad, nothing could hurt me. And now, this eerie feeling nudged me to think that maybe there was something of value to my dad's entering an alcohol rehabilitation center. I'm not sure how I was able to feel that eerie sensation because I had so much anger and resentment built up and I was always high. It had to be a power greater than myself.

My dad completed his treatment program and was released thirty days after entering rehab. While he started attending twelve-step meetings and living a sober life, my world had collapsed. The epitome of this was when my wife moved out with the kids and then the drug dealers took everything I owned.

I sat in the empty apartment feeling sorry for myself for a while. I didn't know what to do. At that point, I did not yet realize I had a problem with drugs and alcohol, but the problem of a place to live was obvious. I decided I needed to go to my dad's house and ask him for help. I had to hitchhike there because my bicycle was gone too, and I did not have a car or a driver's license. I left my apartment without looking back. I stuck out my thumb. Immediately, a car pulled over. I ran to jump in, but some guy stuck his head out of the passenger window and said, "So long sucker."

The car sped off. I felt cursed. I could not understand why my life had to always be messed up. Their prank compounded my feeling of emptiness. It took every ounce of mental stamina I had left to convince myself to continue hitchhiking. A few cars later, I got a ride to my dad's town and walked the rest of the way.

When I got to his front door, I hesitated out of fear and thought about running away. But there was nowhere to run. After contemplating for several minutes, with my hair disheveled and my face sunken, I finally knocked. My dad answered the door.

"Hi, Dad. How are you?"

My dad had only been out of rehab for a few weeks, but he looked good. His complexion had a healthy glow. He had a nervous look on his face when he saw me. "I'm okay. How are you?" he replied.

Unsure what to say, I just stared at him briefly until the words came to me. I finally said, "I owe some bad people money. They just took all my stuff, and Racquel left a few weeks ago."

For the first time in a long time, my dad was not under the influence of alcohol. There was a pause. It felt like an hour, but it was only about ten seconds. "Well, come in and fix yourself something to eat."

After I finished eating a sandwich, I sat down with him in the living room. He didn't pester me with questions or drill me with advice. Instead, he said, "Let's watch this movie together. It's called *Hoosiers*." Interestingly, the movie was about a high school basketball team winning the state championship. One of the players' fathers was a drunk who wound up in a sanitarium to dry out.

My dad agreed to let me stay there, telling me, "I think you should attend a twelve-step meeting."

Just to be agreeable, I said, "Sure, Dad, I'll go to one."

But in my mind, I didn't think I had a problem with drugs and alcohol.

For my first meeting, I arrived fifteen minutes late and left ten minutes early. It didn't take long to decide that twelve-step groups were not for me.

When I got back, my dad asked, "Rob, did you go to a meeting?"

I replied, "Yeah, it was okay." I just wanted to please my dad.

Meanwhile, Racquel and the kids had moved back into our apartment. Her mother helped her get situated. Racquel applied to social services and received the necessary aid to stay there. After two months of living with my dad, I decided I wanted to move back home with her. I hitched a ride to the apartment. When I arrived, I was shocked to find another man living there. I lost my mind. Anger took hold, and I began to shake. I grabbed him by the neck and slammed him up against the wall. He broke loose from my grip and escaped out the front door. The kids were still asleep in the bedroom with Racquel.

Upon seeing me, Racquel clenched her jaw, and with angry red face, she screamed, "Rob, we are done!"

While I was aware that I had been a horrible husband and father, it still hurt deeply to know she was with someone else.

"I can't believe you're with another guy!" I yelled.

"What do you care?" she yelled back.

I slammed the front door and left. I knew if I stayed, I was going to hurt someone.

I unraveled. I had been working and saving money while at my dad's. My thought was to move back home and patch things up. Now that the plan had exploded, I took the money I had saved and bought an ounce of weed and a brand-new Colnago racing bicycle. Within a few days, I was back to using drugs and alcohol daily, hiding it from my dad. It wasn't hard for him to notice that I was using again. He had been sober for about six months and understood addiction a lot better.

One day, he sat me down and said, "Rob, if you are using again, you can't stay here."

With a blank stare, I replied, "I'm not using."

We both knew it was a lie.

Unable to shake my anger that Racquel had a new boyfriend, I convinced myself that I was going to buy a gun and murder him. Slowly, I had eased back into selling drugs and making connections. My older brother, knowing I was having a hard time, called and asked, "Why don't you pack up your stuff and move down here to Miami, Florida? Bring your Colnago. They have lots of club races in the industrial parks."

"I think that's a good idea." My anger was plaguing me constantly, day and night, and I couldn't help but admit, "If I stay here, I think I will kill Raquel's boyfriend."

In an eager voice, he replied, "Come down here and cool off. Maybe you can get situated and work things out with Racquel."

I arrived in Miami a few days later. My brother let me stay with him and got me a job at the Port of Miami. It was great. I loved the warm weather and all the palm trees. Everything was going well.

Early on, I told Ben. "I can drink beer and smoke weed, but I have to stay away from hard liquor and cocaine."

He nodded in agreement.

Ben signed me up for a local bicycle race a few days after I got there. It was in an industrial park, and they did mile laps. On the way to the race, I was drinking a Corona beer and smoking a joint.

Ben's business partner and best friend, Jamie, asked, "Should you be drinking beer and smoking weed before a bicycle race?"

I responded, "I'll race better," and then started laughing. I took third in the race and won my first bicycle racing trophy.

Unfortunately, my new life in Miami began to crumble. It was my pattern of self-destruction. I couldn't escape it. It followed me everywhere. Ben and I were shooting nine-ball at a pool hall one day. We ordered a pitcher of beer and started our game.

Then, Ben got a call and said, "I gotta go. I'll be back in a few hours. Don't go anywhere!"

Before he could return, I met someone who had crack cocaine. The chance meeting sent me on a two-day cocaine run.

Eventually, I turned up in Opa Locka, Florida, at a crack house not too far from Miami. I don't remember much about that journey. I left that house and decided I would hitchhike back to New York. I got a ride to North Miami Beach.

Before dropping me off, the guy said, "Listen, hitchhiking on I-95 is serious business. I've watched people get run over. Be careful."

I shook his hand and said, "Thanks, I will be." By then, I was coming down off my crack high and had a little common sense. I wandered into North Miami Beach looking for a pay phone. I saw a picture of Michael Keaton advertising the movie, *Clean and Sober*, on the side of a bus stop. For whatever reason, I walked up to it and punched Michael in the face. I hit it so hard that all my knuckles were bleeding. I found a pay phone and called Ben.

"Hey. Can you come get me? I'm in North Miami Beach," I mumbled into the phone.

"Bro. I've been worried sick about you. I thought you were dead," he replied.

"Nope, I'm still alive."

"Look for a number on one of the buildings."

I told him where I was.

"I'll be there in an hour," he uttered fearfully. Then, almost screaming at me, he added, "Don't go anywhere. I'll be there!"

When Ben found me, I could tell he had been formulating what he would say to me. After we got into the car, we sat there for a few seconds.

He finally looked over at me and calmly stated, "Bro. I love you, but you can't stay here anymore. We have to call dad." I had only been there for about four months.

Feeling unable to argue, I agreed and said, "Okay, let's call him."

We stopped at a liquor store on the way home. I told Ben I needed a bottle of Jack Daniels to calm down after my two-day crack run.

A few days later, Ben put me on a Greyhound back to New York. I arrived at my dad's house in October of 1988 with all my belongings in a garbage bag. I left my Colnago racing bicycle behind. I could not bring it on the bus.

My dad commanded, "This is your last chance to stay here. If you start using drugs and alcohol again, I have to put you out. Do you understand?"

I told him I understood. But I kept using. However, on November 25, 1988, about a month after I arrived at my dad's house, a miracle happened. I was with a friend, betting on the horse races at the harness track. I had a big bag of weed and a six-pack of beer. Like always, we parked the car at the far end of the racetrack near the final turn for the last race of the night. When the race ended, we didn't have a single winning ticket.

My friend shook his head in disgust. We don't have any winning tickets so let's smoke a joint before we leave."

I didn't want to. I didn't question it and didn't think it was strange. It was like some higher power zapped me of the desire to get high.

With confidence, I said, "I'm done. I don't want to get high anymore. I can't live like this." I handed my bag of weed to him and said, "Here, you can have it."

I haven't had a drink or a drug since.

He replied, "Oh, shush. I don't want your weed."

"I'm serious; take it. Take the beer, too."

With a suspicious expression he said, "Okay, I'll hold on to it for you."

The next morning, November 26, 1988, I approached my dad and asked him if we could talk.

He replied, "Yes, son. What's going on?"

Without making eye contact, I choked out, "I haven't been honest with you. I've been using drugs and alcohol for the last month. But last night, something happened. A voice in my head told me to stop using. I have a problem, and I need help."

My dad hesitated and looked at me with a knowing look. "I knew you were using. I found all your liquor and beer bottles in the basement. But I do hear in your voice that you are sincere about getting help."

Dad's first step to get help for me was to get me on his insurance plan, but that failed. He didn't have enough cash to pay for my treatment but searched for other ways to cover the cost. We both applied to several rehab centers, but none of them would offer me admission without insurance to cover it. It seemed like a lost cause.

I continued to attend twelve-step meetings and stayed away from my old friends. My desire to stay clean and sober was sincere. I had had enough. For the first time since forever, I wanted to do the right thing. My dad and I were both discouraged about me not getting into a rehab program, but my dad consistently reminded me that all would be well and to trust the process. Almost out of the blue, I received a call from a Catholic Rehab Center, Pius XII. It was only a few miles from my dad's house.

"Hi, this is Gene Brush. We see that Robert Woods submitted an application to our rehabilitation program. Can I speak with him?"

"This is Robert."

Gene eagerly stated, "I am pleased to let you know that you have been accepted into our program, and because of your hardship, we are charging one dollar a week."

I didn't know what to say. After an awkward, pregnant pause, I sputtered, "Okay, what do I need to do?"

He said, "Show up on Monday and ask for Janice. She will be your primary counselor."

"Thank you so much. I will see you on Monday," I replied. It was a true miracle. God was doing for me what I could not do for myself. Only, at the time, I did not realize it yet.

On Monday, I showed up at the rehabilitation center not knowing what to expect. I had not used any drugs or alcohol in over a week. My hands were sweaty and shaky. I wanted to run away from that place as fast as I could, but somehow, I knew my running away days were over. I rang the buzzer, and my counselor, Janice, answered the door. Janice greeted me with a warm smile. She was dressed professionally and was wearing a lot of jewelry. Her warm presence helped me get over my nervousness.

"Come in," she said. "You must be Robert."

With a nervous smile, I replied, "Yes, I'm Robert. I was told to be here at 9:00."

She beamed. "Yup, and you're right on time. Follow me."

I followed her down a hallway and into her office.

"Have a seat," she directed.

I sat down and stared at the posters she had on the wall. It reminded me of all the times I had sat in the principal's office at school. One of the posters read, "The mind is a terrible thing to waste." Another read, "The thousand-mile journey begins with the first step."

As we settled in, Janice addressed me kindly with an outstretched hand. "I've been assigned to be your counselor. I'm going to do your intake. It means I'm going to ask you a lot of questions."

It took over an hour. She asked questions about my childhood, my siblings, my parents, my wife and kids, and my drug and alcohol use. Even though I was twenty-five years old and had been to hell and back, I still felt like a little child. Janice was amazing and was a perfect fit to be my counselor. I needed a soft, compassionate, and understanding demeanor to get through this process. Janice had all those qualities.

Toward the end of the intake, she stopped, took a breath, looked me in the eye, and asked, "Robert, have you ever been sexually abused?"

It felt like someone had punched me in the stomach. Heat rose up my neck, and I could feel my face redden. I began to panic. The weight of the question made me feel as though I couldn't breathe. I felt like I had to run out of there so I could get some air.

But instead, I looked her in the eye and lied, "No."

I could tell she knew it was a lie, but she did not ask me again. I couldn't say it, talk about it, or acknowledge it.

After the intake, Janice said, "Robert, I recommended you for our eighteen-month program. I will put together your treatment plan, which we will discuss. I will adjust it as you get better. Do you have any questions or concerns for me?"

Emotionally bankrupt and raw, I could not express my feelings. I sat there silently for a few minutes, not knowing how to respond.

Finally, I spoke tentatively, "I don't want to talk in front of people. It makes me nervous." Janice had commented during the intake that I would be sitting in groups and going out to twelve-step meetings.

Janice nodded, showing approval. She completely understood me. She handed me a paper that had about fifteen different faces. The faces represented feelings, with an angry face, a sad face, a disgusted face, a lonely face, and so on.

I took the paper.

"Identify what you are feeling and just begin with 'I.' Rob, you have nothing to be afraid of. It's perfectly normal. In time, it will get better. *You* will get better. I promise." She explained further by adding, "Make 'I' statements, like 'I feel really scared sitting in this meeting,' or 'I am afraid to share in meetings.'"

Janice taught me how to take care of my emotional self, something I hadn't done in a very long time. I felt optimistic.

The treatment was miraculous. For the first time in my life, I began to open up and let people into the crazy world inside my head. I learned that I was not a bad person trying to be good, but a sick person trying to get well. I learned that I had a disease called addiction and that it was a family disease. Getting better was a slow process, but I had the will to stay and work to improve. Even though I couldn't talk about the abuse part of my life, Janice helped me tremendously.

One day in a group, about twenty of us were sitting in a circle. The counselor assigned to run the group that day, not Janice, got everyone's attention and said, "Look around the room. Get a good look at each other. Only two of you will make it. The rest of you will die or relapse."

I thought to myself, "I'm one of the two. I wonder who the other one will be." I wanted recovery badly.

Following that group, I had an individual session with Gene, the counselor who called to tell me I had been accepted into the program.

Gene said, "Rob, we are going to work on your first step prep." He explained to me that the first step prep was a diary of my life, and that it was up to me, after I had written my story, whether I wanted to continue with self-destructive behaviors. He added, "Please don't lie, because you are lying to yourself. You are looking for the opportunity to make a rational decision about the direction of your life."

Without trepidation, I nodded. "Gene, I'm all in. I've been self-destructing for the last fifteen years. I don't want to live like that anymore."

After the first step prep, Gene asked, "Rob, what do you want to do with your life? What are your dreams and passions? What do you do to have fun?"

They were great questions, questions I had not asked myself in a long time. Immediately, I thought of my bicycle and how I wanted to become a professional cyclist. I glued a picture of Greg LeMond climbing the Alp d'Huez in the Tour de France on the front of my first step prep folder. I thought about being a responsible husband and father. I thought about going back to school and getting an education.

Treatment and recovery gave me a lot of hope, and it gave me direction. Even though my counselors reinforced the concept of staying away from certain people, places, and things, I did go back to some of my old friends. I wanted them to know about my new way of life. But they didn't care. They even offered to get me high. It was a good learning experience because I decided to stay away from old friends and make new friends who were clean and sober. It's called a sober network. I learned to rely on them. Slowly, I was building a strong foundation for my new sober life.

My first Colnago, 1988. My friend, Pat, and me getting ready to go for a ride.

CHAPTER TEN

GED to PhD

"I am not afraid of storms, for I am learning how to sail my ship."

- Louisa May Alcott

Part of my treatment plan in rehab was to get a high school diploma and possibly attend college. Janice and I met weekly to discuss my treatment progress. I looked forward to those meetings and felt grateful for Janice being my counselor.

At one of our weekly meetings, Janice asked, "Robert, how do you feel about going back to school and getting your diploma and possibly going to college?"

I just looked at her with a huge smile on my face.

"What's the smile about?"

"One time, I almost got arrested for drugs, and it scared me. That day, I told my friend Felix that I wanted to go back to school," I explained. I then told her the story.

I was sitting at my kitchen table preparing to repackage a large quantity of drugs I had just bought. I had posted my friend Felix at my front door. He was the lookout and would stop anyone from rushing through the door.

He heard a knock and loudly asked, "Who is it?"

"The police," a lady's voice responded.

I froze. Then, in an instant, I shoved all my drugs in the freezer. My friend opened the door but stood in front of the doorway. He didn't let the police officer inside.

"Is that your car parked in the no-parking spot across the street?" she asked.

"Yes, I will move it right now," Felix barked back.

I sat down at my kitchen table, sweat beading on my forehead, and I could feel my rapid heartbeat. I wiped the sweat with my arm and thought, "That was a close call." I sat at the table, staring into space. For that split second, I knew that if the cops raided my house, I would be in jail for a long time. I bought drugs so many times without fear, but for whatever reason, this experience forced me to reflect.

I said aloud, "I don't want to go to jail."

Before this episode, I had been reflecting on how I wanted to get out of this lifestyle, but I was in too deep to just walk away. It was my only source of income, and I owed drug dealers money. It was a vicious cycle. A regular nine-to-five job would not have provided enough income to erase my debt on the street.

I paused for a few seconds, and Janice asked, "What happened next?"

I explained that I sat there for a few minutes processing the close call. I remembered drifting back to a time before my drug habit, when I liked school and envisioned a brighter future.

I was in the second grade and loved going to school.

One day, I cried to my mom, "How come Mary Alice and Ben get homework and I don't?"

My mom looked at me with a half grin and shook her head. "Be patient. You will have homework soon enough."

"Mom, what does patient mean?" I asked.

"It means to relax and wait for your turn," she explained. "You'll be their age soon and get homework. Then you will complain about having too much homework."

I still wanted homework, but I sort of understood what she was saying.

"Okay, I'll be patient. But I still want homework," I grumbled.

"Go find a book out of the dining room and read it."

I ran into the dining room and picked out *Tom Sawyer* by Mark Twain. I ran back to my mother and asked, "Is this okay to read?"

"Absolutely! You will like that story."

I couldn't wait to begin reading it. The next day, I showed my teacher the book I was reading, and he said, "Robert, that's a great book. I'm glad you like to read."

I made eye contact with Janice and said, "That close call made me wish I could go back to my second-grade self and redo so much since then."

Janice, who was attentively listening, asked, "How did the situation unfold?"

I reflected for a few seconds and continued telling the story.

The front door opened and closed. Felix had returned from parking his car and saw me sitting at the table.

He asked, "Are you okay?"

"Yeah, that was a close call. I was just thinking about

how messed up it would have been if they raided the house. I would have been going away for a long time," I told him.

"Yeah, that would have sucked," Felix replied.

"It made me think about when I used to like going to school. I want to get out of the drug game and go back to school. I know I could do it if I got the chance," I explained.

Felix nodded his head in agreement. "Yeah, I don't know how I got into this racket. I sometimes think about living a normal life. My mom and dad didn't give a crap about me. I dropped out when I was sixteen and never even thought about going back. Maybe you can get out of this crazy life and go back to school someday."

His response gave me hope. I told him, "I was smart when I was young. I was reading and writing before I went to kindergarten. My parents encouraged us to read the classics. School was always so easy. My mom said I was assessed at the genius level when I took the IQ test. After my parents split up, I hated school."

"Yeah, I know the feeling," Felix replied.

Felix and I finished prepping the drugs for distribution that day but soon lost touch. He saved my butt by standing in front of the doorway.

I smiled at Janice. "I'm glad I didn't get arrested. Now I'm sitting with you discussing the possibility of going back to school."

"I'm glad you told me that story. I am recommending going back to school as part of your plan," Janice rejoiced.

I continued smiling. "I've always wondered what it would be like to go back to school."

"Well, now you have the chance."

"I'm really happy about that."

I had a sound, well-thought-out treatment plan. I was focused, and I wanted to get better. I followed the plan and did everything Janice and the other counselors recommended. When I attended the GED preparation class, I asked a lot of questions. I studied whenever I had the chance. For the first time in a long time, it felt good to read and write. My brain was clear.

During one of my individual sessions with Janice, she took both of my hands and stared into my eyes. "Robert, you are ready to take the GED exam. I signed you up for it. It is a two-day exam."

I squeezed Janice's hands and felt the sensation of joy. I looked back into her eyes and gleefully stated, "I still can't believe I have the opportunity to get my high school diploma. I thought this day would never come."

I took the exam and felt confident that I did well. A few months later, I received a brown envelope in the mail from the New York State Education Department. I knew it was the results of my test. I held it but didn't want to open it. I took it with me to a twelve-step meeting I was required to attend. I told my sponsor, Sean, that I was afraid to open it.

He asked, "Rob, what are you afraid of? If you failed it, you just take it again."

With trepidation, I slowly began opening it. In the envelope was my General Equivalency Diploma. My GED. Essentially, I just graduated high school.

Sean took it and shouted to the room, "Hey everybody, Rob got his GED!"

Everyone clapped. I was glowing.

The next day, I showed Janice.

"Robert, I am so proud of you! You are doing so well with your treatment," she cried out excitedly.

I smiled. "I can't believe I have my GED. Everyone thought I'd be dead before I hit the age of twenty-one. I never thought it was possible."

"You are a miracle," she replied.

Taking a moment to reflect, I sat silently. I was learning about feelings, and I knew what I felt in that moment. "I feel grateful."

With a look of encouragement, Janice said, "Well, I have more good news. I recommended you for a program called Adult Education Program and Policy (AEPP). They will pay for you to go to college for one full-time semester. And you were accepted."

With a bewildered look on my face, I nervously replied, "I'm learning all about these feelings. When you mentioned college, I felt scared."

"Robert, you will do great."

I went to day rehab and college night classes while living with my dad and stepmom. I came home from my English 101 class one day and said, "Dad, I'm in trouble. This class is hard. I don't think I'm going to make it."

"Son, I'll help you through it," my dad stated with devotion.

I explained the assignment to him. I had to write an expository essay. And I had no idea what that meant.

My dad explained, "An expository essay means you are providing your audience with factual information. It is best to do a compare and contrast style."

"Okay, I'll use my textbook to help me," I replied.

I sat down for a few hours and wrote my first essay. I

had a week to complete it because evening classes were once a week. I asked my dad to look it over.

He said, "Son, you have to work on your handwriting. I can hardly read it."

"I know. It will take some practice for sure."

The assignment came back with red ink all over it and comments that said, "Please type your papers. It's a struggle to read your work." And at the very top of the paper was the letter grade, D-minus.

The professor said to the entire class, "Read my comments and make the necessary edits. I will regrade it and take the average of the two assignments."

I sat there sulking. I had put hours into that assignment, and he gave me a D-minus. I knew for sure that he had it out for me.

I showed my dad the paper and told him how mad I was.

My dad simply replied, "Make the edits and keep trying."

I made the necessary edits and turned it in. The next assignment was another essay, but I worked harder this time. I did not have a typewriter, so I took my time and wrote it as neatly as possible. Handing it to my dad, I asked, "Can you look this over again and give me some suggestions?"

"Sure, and your handwriting looks a little better," he replied.

"Thanks for helping me, Dad."

With a proud smile on his face, he said, "You're welcome. I'm glad I can help, and I'm glad we are able to spend time together." Dad was starting to be my mentor again.

I went up to my room and sat on the edge of my bed,

thinking, "I'm glad that my dad and I are spending time together doing homework. We missed a lot of that time after he left home. And now we have a second chance."

That became our routine. I'd work on an essay, he'd make suggestions, and I would turn in my essay after hours of hard work. Each time, my professor returned it with red ink comments all over it and a D-minus at the top.

One day, I stopped at the supermarket after class to buy some ice cream. I wasn't using drugs and alcohol, but I used sugar. As I stood in line waiting to pay, I saw my English 101 professor walk into the store. I thought, "There's that asshole. He doesn't like me and keeps giving me low scores on my papers. I'm gonna wait for him outside and knock him out."

I paid for my ice cream and waited outside for him. My hands were sweaty, and my heart was racing. The more I thought about it, all the long hours I had put into my essays, the more I wanted to punch him. I saw him get in line and thought, "Great, here he comes. I'm gonna give him just what he deserves. A fist to his face."

He paid for his stuff, and I watched him come out of the door. As I started to approach him, I heard Janice's voice in my head. *Robert, I'm proud of you. You're going to do great.* In an instant, I walked away and never confronted him. He never knew what I had planned.

This was a real growth moment for me. My old self would have relished the opportunity to beat up my professor. However, my maturing persona saw the benefit in leaving it alone.

I loved my other classes. Math wasn't my favorite subject, but I was good at it. Sociology and psychology were interesting. My sociology professor once told me, "Robert, I liked your essay. How did you learn to write good essays?"

"Thank you. I put a lot of time into my assignments, and my English professor taught me," I replied.

At that moment, I realized my English 101 professor did not have it out for me. He set the bar high and gave me and the other students sound instructions on writing college essays. It was never personal. I had to retrain my brain from the world I had come from, where everyone tried to exploit my weaknesses. I had to learn how to open up to others, to be receptive to people who were trying to help me. I was so grateful I had not beaten up my English professor. He was hard on me for a reason. He wanted me to be successful in college. Because of his high expectations, I was now able to write formulated essays.

I finished the four classes but had to repeat English 101. I received a D-minus in the class overall. Instead of being mad, I was glad to take English again. But this time it was with a different professor. I wanted to improve my writing skills. I passed this time with a B.

I kept the momentum going and applied to a state university. They offered associate and bachelor's degree programs. I was accepted and matriculated into a two-year degree program, an associate's in human services. My plan was to complete the program and continue on to acquire a bachelor's degree in social work. At the same time, I was offered a job in a juvenile detention center for adolescent boys.

A few weeks later, my ex-wife called and asked, "Can the boys live with you?" She was having a hard time making ends meet.

There was no other answer but yes. I became a single dad, worked a full-time job, and started as a full-time student. I had no idea how I'd manage it all. But I did. I requested the overnight shift at work. I had to do bed checks, call central control, and report accountability for all the boys on my block. In between bed checks, I did my homework. People close to me looked after the boys at night. It took a lot of adjustments for me and my boys to settle in together, but we established a rhythm.

My oldest son was ten, my middle son was eight, and the twins were six. I had a two-bedroom apartment, and we were all learning to live together. They went to school during the day, and I slept. I'd be awake when they got home, and I would bring them with me to my evening college classes.

One night, when we arrived at one of my classes, I instructed the boys, "You guys sit outside of my classroom and work on your homework. If you need me, get my attention, and I'll come out."

They all understood the routine. That night was my night for giving a presentation. I hated to talk in front of the class. Just the thought of it made my insides tremble.

When I heard, "Up next, Robert Woods," I stood up with sweaty palms, a racing heartbeat, and a dry mouth. I needed water but didn't have any. I stood in front of the class and tried to clear my throat. It did not make my nervousness go away.

I mumbled my first few words, but before I even got started, I heard, "Dad?" I looked around. One of the twins was walking toward me, saying, "Can I sharpen my pencil?"

The class laughed, and my professor smiled.

"Sure," I said.

I walked him over to the pencil sharpener, sharpened his pencil, and brought him back out to the hallway. I got a C on the presentation, but the grade didn't really matter. My boys and I found a way to grow up together.

Life was a struggle, but we lived it together. My twelve-step sponsor helped me with my sober life and the direction of my education. I called him one day, saying, "I got my associate's degree in human services, but I don't think I want to be a social worker like you."

He was not offended and asked, "What are you thinking about?"

"I'm not sure. I think I want to become a teacher, but I'm afraid to talk in front of people."

He laughed and said, "Don't worry about it. With practice, you'll gain confidence. Make an appointment to meet with your academic advisor and tell her you want to change your plan of study."

Two years later, I received my bachelor's degree in education and became a certified social studies teacher.

I never, in a million years, imagined that I would become a teacher. In September 1998, I drove for an hour to start my first day as a middle school teacher. I was hired by a Roman Catholic school to teach the sixth, seventh, and eighth-grade social studies and religion classes. Halfway into the drive, the lid on my coffee fell off, and I spilled most of it down the middle of my shirt. I stopped at a gas station, washed the shirt, and stood under a hand dryer. I got most of it, but it was still noticeable. Battling the negative monster (the lunatic) in my head, I continued the drive.

I said aloud, "I'm going to work whether I am nervous

or not. I'm facing my fears and will teach these kids to the best of my ability."

My classroom was all set up. My mom had made me a beautiful set of curtains for my closets, and I had decorated all the bulletin boards. I walked up to the chalkboard and wrote my name on it with the date. I got a tingling feeling in my stomach. I still couldn't believe I was a schoolteacher. I stood there for a moment and thought, "Sixth grade was when my world fell apart. I couldn't imagine any one of my students going through what I went through at that age."

Before I got lost in my thoughts, I heard, "Are you Mr. Woods?"

"Yes, I am. Good morning," I replied cheerfully.

"Good morning," the student replied. "This is my homeroom class. Do you have a seating arrangement?"

I hesitated and realized that I had never considered a seating chart. "No, sit wherever you like."

Another student entered and said, "Good morning, Mr. Woods. What happened to your shirt?"

Chuckling, I instantly thought about how kids often don't hold back what comes to mind and replied, "Oh, I spilled my coffee on the way to work."

She said, "That stinks. My dad does it all the time."

And little by little, my classroom began to fill with sixth-grade students.

I knew I had found the right calling. I loved to teach. At the end of my third year, the students dedicated the student yearbook to me and named me Teacher of the Year. I was speechless. At the same time, my colleagues kept encouraging me to become the principal.

The seventh-grade teacher told me, "Rob, you should

become the principal. You are the glue that holds the upper grades together."

"No way! I love to teach!" I quickly replied.

A few days later, one of my students' parents said, "Mr. Woods, we need you to become the school principal."

I laughed. "My colleague said that to me, too."

After hearing the sentiment a few more times, I decided to explore the possibility of going to school for educational leadership.

By this time, I had already acquired an associate's, bachelor's, and master's degree in education. I yielded to the call to become an administrator and applied to a program at a state university about an hour from my house, the Certificate of Advanced Study in Academic Leadership. I was accepted and absolutely loved the program. Most of the classes required me to connect with local school districts and to have discussions with current administrators. It was a hands-on program mixed with study.

During the final semester, before I graduated, the department chair approached me with a compliment. "Robert, you are an excellent student with a lot of potential. Have you ever thought about becoming a school lawyer or getting your doctorate?"

I smiled. "No, I haven't. I didn't really want to do this program, but all my colleagues and my students' parents kept telling me to become the principal of the school."

"Well, give it some thought," she suggested.

I couldn't help but wonder to myself, "How did I ever get this far?"

Graduating fourth in my class and receiving the highest degree the university offered, a Certificate of Advanced

Study (CAS), I decided I would attend graduation. I had elected not to attend graduation ceremonies for my other degrees. I didn't see the point. At that time, I thought, "The reason for college is to get a degree, not to go to a ceremony." I called my mom, my stepdad, my dad, and my stepmom and invited all of them to attend.

My dad beamed. "I've waited a long time for this day to come."

I thought a lot about what the department chair told me: "Have you ever thought about becoming a school lawyer or getting your doctorate?" I loved law and taught civics in middle school. However, I did not know anything about a doctorate degree. A few months after I graduated, I researched both and decided to go for my doctorate. I applied to an online accredited PhD program that offered a doctorate in education. I was accepted. They assigned me a mentor who was also the chair of my doctoral committee. Dr. Keen, who preferred to be addressed as Cheryl, was the perfect selection. Cheryl, a Harvard graduate, was a lot like that English 101 professor. She had high expectations and played a huge role in the direction of my studies.

CHAPTER ELEVEN

More Doubt than Faith

"Jesus reached out his hand and caught him. 'You of little faith,' he said, 'why did you doubt?'"

- MATTHEW 14:31 (NIV)

As I BECAME sober, I self-reflected a lot. I began to notice situations that I believed were God's intervention in my life. All the interactions with Mrs. Leap were significant even when I questioned whether God existed or even cared about my well-being.

When my mom was hospitalized with ulcers, God's silver lining was Deacon Don. Deacon Don was an Episcopal deacon who visited the hospital to comfort the sick. He visited my mom each week, and they became friends. When my mom recovered, they continued their friendship and began dating. My mom's spiritual health improved, too. Before long, my mom married Deacon Don. She finally had a chance to be happy again.

Meeting Deacon Don, in hindsight, was an obvious sign of God working in my mom's life, my siblings' lives, and mine, too. Don had a positive influence on all of us. At the time, I did not recognize it was the hand of God.

During my early years of sobriety, late 1988, early 1989, my mom and stepdad, Deacon Don, invited me to attend church with them on Sundays. I accepted and joined them when I could. I enjoyed it and found it comforting. It was as if I knew I was supposed to be at church.

One Sunday, after church, I sat in the pews staring at Jesus on the cross.

My mom grabbed her purse and said to me, "Come on, son. Are you ready to go?"

"I'll be out in a few minutes. I'm gonna sit here a minute."

"Okay, Don is talking with Father JoÚ. Meet us at the car."

I nodded my head in agreement and sat there in the empty church, staring at the cross. I thought, "It's so awesome that I'm going to church with my mom." For about fifteen seconds, I felt a peace beyond understanding. It was better than any drug I had ever taken. The experience had such an impact on me that I sought help for discernment.

A few days later, I spoke to the priest. I sat in his office, looking at all the icons and smelling the freshly burnt incense. The aroma helped me relax.

He asked, "Robert, what can I do for you?"

A little embarrassed I answered him, "I think God wants me to become a priest."

Father JoÚ hesitated, cleared his throat, and asked, "Why do you think that?"

"Because the other day, after church, I felt a peace

beyond my understanding. It was a better feeling than any drug I have ever taken."

He replied, "Let's see what God has in mind. To become a priest, you must have at least a bachelor's degree, so we have some time to discern."

I felt dejected and looked down at the floor. "I don't even have my high school diploma." I looked up at him with a hopeful look, "I am in treatment. My counselor recommended getting a high school diploma and possibly going to college. I do have some time to discern."

With a calm, confident voice, Father JoÚ said, "Let's meet once a month and talk about your spiritual walk."

I agreed, and Father JoÚ became my spiritual advisor.

Slowly, in early 1989, all the broken pieces of my life began to heal. It seemed strange to dismiss the idea that something divine didn't have a hand in it. I said yes to the voice in my head that told me to stop using drugs. After my yes, little doors continued to open, and I was finally walking through them. I really started to believe that God had a hand in all of it. But it was a minimal amount of faith. Even though I had more doubt than faith in God, Janice, my counselor, kept reminding me to trust the process and once said, "Doubt the doubt, not the faith."

When I was ready for the next step in my sober journey, selecting a sponsor, Janice guided me through the process. She explained that a sponsor is someone who will take you through the twelve steps and guide you through recovery. However, Janice was adamant that men sponsor men and women sponsor women. When I got the courage to ask someone to be my sponsor, a man named Sean, it turned out he was Catholic.

I saw Sean at a lot of twelve-step meetings. He had been sober for a few years and had an outgoing personality. I liked that about him.

After he agreed to be my sponsor, I heard him share in a meeting, "I'm an Irish Catholic from the Bronx."

Sean took me to a lot of meetings and helped me form a sober network. He encouraged me to spend time with sober men; we would watch fights on television, play basketball, and go to the diner after meetings. It didn't take long to establish some real friendships. And most importantly, I had made my first true friend in sobriety. I had a friend who genuinely cared about me.

Around ten months into my sobriety, Sean got really sick. I did not know that he had contracted HIV from intravenous drug use. He told me when his HIV progressed to AIDS. He got too sick to attend meetings or even hang out. His dad, who also attended our twelve-step meetings as a recovering alcoholic, approached me one night after a meeting. With his Irish brogue, he said, "Robert, I'm not sure how this is going to turn out for Sean. I love him with all my heart. I'm making a pilgrimage to Our Lady of Medjugorje. I will pray for Sean's healing while I'm there."

Those words startled me. I thought about Mrs. Leap taking my prayer to the Grotto in Lourdes, France. I hadn't thought about that in a long time.

I didn't know how to respond to Sean's dad, but with a soft voice, I said, "I've heard about apparitions of the Blessed Virgin Mary. My friend's mom went to Our Lady of Lourdes before I got sober. She left a prayer I wrote on a piece of paper at the Grotto." After a pause, I added, "I'm so sorry. Sean is my best friend. He helps me so much. Is there anything I can do to help?"

He put his hand on my shoulder, "Yes, Robert, there are a couple of things you can do for our Sean. Pray for him. And take him to daily Mass when you can. He can no longer drive."

"I'd be glad to take him. And I certainly will pray for him," I assured.

One of the benefits of my recovery and part of my treatment plan was to get a driver's license. My dad taught me to drive, and I took my road test with his New Yorker a few months after I got sober. I took Sean to Mass whenever I could. I looked forward to my time with Sean and attending Mass.

One day, I took Sean to a daily Mass. When it came time for communion, I got up to get in line. Sean stopped me, saying, "Rob, you can't receive communion if you're not Catholic."

He handed me the prayerbook provided by the parish, called a missalette, and showed me the caption that explained the process for non-Catholics. The caption stated that non-Catholics were not properly prepared to receive the Eucharist, the Body and Blood of Jesus Christ. Sean explained, "Catholics believe that the bread and wine are transformed into the actual holy body and blood of Jesus."

I felt sad and rejected. "Oh, I didn't know that."

Some people may think this exclusionary, but it isn't. Roman Catholics beliefs about the Eucharist are so strong that they believe it is important for people to be educated about it before taking the Sacrament. They are actually protecting non-Catholics from the dire consequences they believe can result from receiving the Eucharist into their bodies without acknowledging its holiness.

When I went to church with my mom and stepdad, there were no stipulations for receiving Holy Communion. In the Episcopal Church, women can be priests, priests can be married, and anyone who has been baptized in the Christian faith can take communion regardless of the denomination.

Sean explained, "Cross your arms, and when you reach the priest. Ask him for a blessing."

I did as he said. The priest made the sign of the cross and touched my head. I went back to the pew and sat in silence. In moments when I felt rejected, I would usually become angry. But this time, it was different. Somehow, in my heart, I knew what Sean was telling me about the bread and wine becoming the body and blood of Christ was true. It was a revelation, an epiphany. I was drawn to want to receive the Eucharist (Holy Communion). Inside, I felt a quiet peace and thought to myself, "I want to become Catholic."

I did not tell anyone about wanting to become Roman Catholic. Not wanting to disappoint Father JoÚ, who was an Episcopalian priest, I kept it to myself. I really didn't understand what was happening, but I did begin to see God working in me. For the first time in my life, I contemplated the existence of God and His plan for me.

Sean's health declined rapidly. He no longer had the strength to walk or get out of bed. He needed a full-time home care aide.

I said to God, "I started to believe in you, that you really care for me, but now, you are taking my friend from me."

I shut down emotionally and closed out the world. I

stopped talking and distanced myself from everyone, including my dad. My doubt increased, and my faith decreased.

My dad was worried and asked, "Is there anyone you can talk to?"

With a somber look, I replied, "I don't want to talk to anyone else. I want Sean to get better."

Up to that point, the closest experience I had with death was watching my mother almost die, but she recovered. Now, I was watching my friend die, and there was nothing I could do. He was admitted to a hospital in New York City.

Eventually, I opened up to my counselors and continued to attend twelve-step meetings. One night after a meeting, I bumped into someone whom I had seen at a lot of the meetings. I knew he had good sobriety. He was engaged in working the twelve steps and attended a lot of meetings. I loved to listen to him share.

Approaching him nervously, I stammered, "Hi, Roger. I'm Robert. Thanks for sharing tonight."

He smiled and, with his Italian New York City accent, said, "You're welcome. How long have you been coming around?"

"Less than a year. I'm in the rehab center in town, and I am required to attend these meetings."

"Oh yeah, I know the place. I speak there occasionally. How's it going?"

"I'm doing well with my treatment, and I attend a lot of twelve-step meetings. But I'm struggling right now. My friend Sean is dying from AIDS."

Roger's eyes teared up. "Sean's a good friend of mine, too. He helped me get sober when I first started coming to meetings. I'm going to visit him tomorrow in the hospital. Do you want to go?"

My heart fluttered, "Absolutely."

We exchanged phone numbers.

"I'll call you tomorrow when I'm on the way to your house."

"Great!" I exclaimed.

We shook hands. I noticed a tag hanging out of his shirt. "Roger, your tag is hanging out of your shirt."

He laughed and said, "No, that's my Brown Scapular. I just started wearing it a few days ago."

I looked at him, a bit stunned.

Roger noticed my reaction and asked, "What's the matter?"

"I've been wearing a Brown Scapular for the last six years." I showed him mine and told him my Brown Scapular story. Roger looked at me with tears rolling down his face.

"I grew up Catholic, and I recently made peace with God. God just gave me a big hug!" We both looked at each other and embraced. I didn't like to be touched, and I certainly did not like to be hugged, but God broke down my wall for that moment with Roger. Roger added, "We'll bring a Brown Scapular down to New York City and put it around Sean."

Roger and I made the trip to see Sean. Sean had developed brain cancer. When we got there, Sean's dad said, "He may not recognize you, but spend time with him anyway."

We entered Sean's room. He recognized us and grinned. He pulled Roger close, struggled through his words, and said, "Please look out for my younger brother."

Roger smiled at him. "Sean, when your brother gets

out of prison, I will take him under my wing. I will look out for him."

Sean smiled back. We could hardly hear him when he talked. He said, "Thanks for coming down. This will be the last time I'll see you guys."

He knew his days were numbered.

"Rob and I brought a Brown Scapular for you. Can we place it on you?" Roger asked.

Sean smiled and nodded his head yes. Roger put the Scapular on him.

Sean died the next day.

On the way home from the hospital, I was quiet. I was still learning how to process feelings, and this was a tough one. Looking over at Roger, I said, "Sean was my sponsor. I'll need another. Will you be my sponsor?"

Roger glanced at me and replied, "I'd be honored to be your sponsor. I want you to call me every day."

While I didn't follow all of Roger's suggestions, I followed the important ones. He said, "Put Post-its on your mirror that read, 'I am a good person' and 'I deserve to feel good.' And say that to yourself every time you look in the mirror." And I listened to this one.

He told me to pray to God every day and to put my meditation books under my bed. He instructed, "When you get on your knees to retrieve them, ask God to keep you sober for the day."

"I can do that," I eagerly responded.

"Good," he replied. "At night, I want you to return your meditation books under your bed. While on your knees, thank God for keeping you sober."

Eventually, I told Roger about my desire to become

Catholic. He smiled and patted me on the shoulder. "I will talk to my priest. In the meantime, you can attend Mass with me." Roger reminded me daily to trust God, clean house, and serve others.

On May 26, 1996, after several months of attending adult conversion classes, I was confirmed into the Roman Catholic Church. Roger was my sponsor then, too. A few days after my confirmation, I called him and asked if we could get together for a talk. Roger had a genuine love for me; I could feel it in my heart. I kept no secrets from him, not even my abuse. Roger told me repeatedly, "You are as sick as your secrets."

He picked me up to attend a twelve-step meeting. We sat in the parking lot before going inside. "You sounded confused when you called me the other day. What's going on?"

"I have come to believe in Jesus Christ as my higher power. I love going to Mass. I love going to meetings. I know God worked and is working miracles in my life, but something is wrong."

He paused for a few seconds and then asked, "What do you mean?"

"I don't cry. I don't show emotion. I have this hardness around my heart that won't allow me to trust people." After a deep breath, I continued, "I pray all the time and do all the right things, but I don't trust God, and I am always full of fear."

Without saying a word, he took my hand and began praying, "Jesus, please remove the hardness surrounding Rob's heart. We know You can do it. Give Rob the willingness to let You."

I didn't become an Episcopal priest, but God was and still is working in my life in many wonderful ways.

Sean on the left and Roger on the right. My sponsors and my first two best friends in recovery.

CHAPTER TWELVE

Let Go and Let God

"Time doesn't heal emotional pain, you need to learn how to let go."

- Roy T. Bennett, *The Light in the Heart*

Professionally, my teaching career was going well. My sobriety was strong, and I knew how to stay clean from drugs and alcohol. My boys were teenagers, all in high school, doing well. We had settled into a sound routine. Life was good. However, subconsciously, I knew my childhood trauma was a major block in my relationship with God and people. But I did not know how to move through it. If I'm being honest, I wasn't ready. I heard in my recovery circles, "Let go and let God, or hang on and get dragged." I did not know how to let go.

Roger knew I was struggling with the hardness of my heart and took action to help me.

"Rob, I signed you up for a three-day Catholic retreat; it's called Cursillo." Cursillo originated in Spain in the 1940s. The emphasis of the weekend was to stress personal spiritual development and for retreatants to take what they learned out into the world. "I think it will be helpful for you," he told me.

After making arrangements for childcare and personal days from work, I called Roger and said, "I'm all set to go. I really want to open my heart to God."

"Great," Roger declared enthusiastically. "I'll pray for you every day you are there. I've asked my church community to pray for you, too!"

Roger drove me to the retreat, praising me for saying yes. When we arrived, Roger put his hand on my shoulder and openly prayed. After he finished praying, he looked me in the eye and said, "Rob, God has a plan for you. I'm sure of it."

The retreatants, all men, were assigned to small groups. My group was called "Fishers of Men." I formed a bond with these men and invited them into my personal world. After sharing some of my internal struggles, I opened up about my lack of trust in God and my inability to show emotion. I also let them know that fear was prominent in my life. Fear controlled my decisions, and I was aware that it was unhealthy and stemmed from a lack of trust. The retreat certainly helped me learn to develop trusting relationships with men.

Each group had a group leader, someone who had already attended the retreat and gave us directions. Ours, Mike, did a great job helping me and the other group members feel relaxed. He was a good listener, funny, and attentive to our needs. I connected with him and asked him for his phone number so the two of us could stay in touch. Mike was more than happy to give me his number. He told me he was thinking about forming a prayer group. The group would meet once a week to share their highs and lows with Jesus. He asked if I was interested. I agreed enthusiastically, thinking it would help me with my current struggles.

Mike followed through, and within a week following the retreat, we formed a prayer group. There were four of us. We developed a strong bond with one another, sharing our personal struggles each week. Two of the members were struggling with pornography. Unsettled, I called Roger and pondered aloud, "I really like my prayer group, and it's helpful for me. I think it's softening my heart. But two guys in the group keep coming back each week, talking about their struggle with pornography, and it makes me uncomfortable. I don't want to hear about it."

With trepidation, Roger lamented, "I understand. But pray for them. They have their struggles just like you have yours."

"I do pray for them!" I declared with frustration in my voice. "But it's irking something inside me. How can someone claim to be following Jesus and then go on their computer and look at that disgusting, disgraceful stuff? I don't get it."

Around the same time, the news revealed incidents of sexual abuse within the Roman Catholic Church between priests and children. There was a particular scandal in the Boston Archdiocese that got my attention. In early 2002, five priests were found guilty of sexual abuse of minors. An additional priest came forward and pled guilty. At first, I thought the media was just trying to increase viewership. But then I read about the enormous payoffs to families and the victims. Not just in the Boston Archdiocese, but nationwide. *The Boston Globe* called their investigation "Spotlight Investigation: Abuse in the Catholic Church." The scandal revealed a pattern of sexual abuse and cover-ups in a large number of archdioceses in the United States. It infuriated me and awakened my childhood trauma. I felt the need to self-destruct and the urge to run away from my responsibilities. I became irritable and agitated often and reacted to minor situations as if they were life or death. Instead of talking to Roger about what was happening to me, I isolated myself.

Slowly, I distanced myself from my Catholic faith and turned to cycling. I raced for a cycling team not far from my house. When I could, I rode with them regularly and participated in races. I became certified to race my track bike on the Vandedrome, a wooden outdoor track designed by JoÚ Vande Velde, a world-renowned track cyclist. Even though I was too old to pursue a career in professional cycling again, it was satisfying to keep up with the cyclists twenty years younger.

I missed Sunday Mass frequently and replaced it with long bike rides. Instead of talking about my feelings and working through them like I had learned, I escaped to my passion for riding bicycles. With the money I saved, I decided to buy a new bike. Instead of talking to Roger about it, I avoided him. I didn't want him to talk me out of it. It was my pattern of self-destruction and avoidance. Getting a new bike helped me deal with my childhood pain twenty-five years ago, so I did it again, hopeful that my old feelings would go away. I bought a Colnago Classic. In my opinion, Colnagos are the finest bicycles ever made. Some people say, the Ferrari's of bicycles.

I left the bicycle shop with my new bike. I felt light on my feet. I couldn't wait to go for a long ride. It was a beautiful shade of light blue, with yellow and orange highlights, my favorite colors. To punch it up, I bought a pair of Vector Pro race wheels that matched perfectly with the frame. I equipped it with Speed Play pedals, recommended by Greg Lemond. I thought, "I'm going to get in the best shape of my life. I'll become an age-group national champion." This was my new focus, instead of dealing with my feelings.

I clicked my cycling shoes into the pedals and pedaled off for a ride. As always, I took it easy for ten miles, making sure I was warmed up and that my seat height was dialed in perfectly. The bike was smooth and fast. By now, I had become a fanatic about my bikes and my rides. The shifting had to be smooth, the wheels perfectly true, the tire pressure exact before every ride, and one water bottle had to have electrolytes and the other one water.

Riding aggressively, I attacked a few climbs and settled into a good tempo. On the next climb, I felt a crick in my neck. I did what I always did when I felt a crick: I moved my head from side to side to adjust my neck. Only this time, when I moved my neck to the right, I heard a *crunch* and felt extreme pain shoot through my neck. By the time I got home, I had lost feeling in my left thumb and index finger.

Eventually, when things didn't get better, I called my brother, who worked with one of the best spine surgeons in the world. "Hey, JoÚ. I was out on a ride a few weeks ago and heard a crunching in my neck. By the time I got home, my left finger and thumb were numb. And they are still numb."

He said, "Well, that sucks. I can confidently say you probably herniated a disc in your cervical spine. It's probably C6, C7. We won't know for sure until you get X-rays and an MRI."

I thought to myself, "Great, I have the best bike I ever owned, and now I can't ride it."

JoÚ turned out to be correct. I had a herniated disc at C6, C7, and a bulging disc at C5, C6. After several consultations with JoÚ and the surgeon, I elected to have a cervical anterior fusion surgery. They entered through the front of my neck and used bone from my hip to fill the titanium cage. A small plate with four screws was used to ensure a strong fusion. I had a three-inch incision with one long suture. The surgeon told me to rest so it could heal properly. However, I couldn't be still. When I stopped, the lunatic came alive.

A week after my surgery, JoÚ called and said, "Hey, bro. How's it going? Any issues with the fusion?"

I updated him on my recovery, saying, "I'm good. My thumb and finger are still numb but it's not stopping me from riding my indoor trainer."

"What the hell is the matter with you? You still have a suture in your neck, and your vertebrae aren't even close to being fused, and you're training indoors!" he screamed.

I laughed. "You know me. I'm a beast on the bike. I can't lose my fitness."

But my brother did not think it was funny. He said, "You have to give your body time to heal. It may take a year."

I sat there thinking about what my brother said. A year is a long time to wait. I thought, "Why does everything in my life have to be so complicated?" And then I thought about the other situations in my life, like walking away from my faith and my avoidance of Roger. Once again, I wasn't letting go. I was getting dragged.

I still wasn't talking to Roger. He did not know that I was not going to Mass regularly or that I was angry with the

Catholic Church and God. He knew about my frustration with my men's prayer group, but I was not honest with him about what was really going on inside. I kept going to my prayer group even though I wanted to quit.

One night, a group member shared, "I slipped again this week. I couldn't help it. It' so easy to go online and look at pornography."

I felt the urge to punch him in the face. I sat there, trying to act empathetic. I could feel my ears turning red. I was getting upset but said nothing.

Another group member said, "Yeah, I can identify with you on how easy it is to look at it. I slipped again this week, too, but God understands."

His response made me feel sick to my stomach. I couldn't take it any longer. I was about to snap. So, I cautiously said, "Sorry, guys. I don't feel well. I have to go."

That was the last time I attended that group. I quit the group and walked away from the Catholic Church.

I was not ready to give up my passion for riding and racing bicycles, and I was definitely not interested in dealing with my trauma. A few months after my cervical fusion surgery, I started racing again. During a club ride, I herniated a disc below my fusion, C5 and C6. I met with JoÚ and the surgeon again and had to have another surgery. This surgery stopped me in my tracks. I didn't realize the severity of the damage I could do by not letting it heal. The severity was clear now.

Roger had moved away to South Carolina shortly after. My communication with him was spotty, so I bottled up a lot of my emotions and problems. Not following the suggestions of the twelve-step program, I didn't get a new sponsor.

I was still clean and sober, but I had all the symptoms of a dry drunk. A dry drunk is someone who displays the same behaviors of an active alcoholic, but is not drinking. In fact, a dry drunk usually becomes angrier.

I cut myself off from all my support systems and stopped going to church altogether. Rather than self-reflect and take time to assess my current situation, I blamed God. I became angry with Him for taking away my ability to ride and race bicycles (and escaping my problems). Tired of my cycling dreams being shattered time and time again, I became bitter and depressed. Every time I pursued cycling, something went wrong. I vowed I would never ride or race again. I'd fix God. Of course, I only hurt myself. Within a few months, I gained over fifty pounds and felt miserable.

I did not understand what was happening and screamed aloud, "God, haven't I had enough pain and suffering? What did I do to deserve this?!" I wanted to jump on my bike and escape, but I couldn't. Sitting on the couch, I dropped my face in my hands but didn't cry. I didn't know how to cry and still hadn't cried a tear in years. After several hours of turmoil, I picked up the phone and called Roger.

"Roger, I'm in a bad way, and I'm not sure what to do. You and I have been praying together for years for God to help me, and I keep coming to a dead end. Now, I can't train anymore, I've gained fifty pounds, I feel like crap, and I'm having suicidal thoughts."

There was a long pause. Roger cleared his throat and finally said, "Rob, I'm so sorry you are going through all of this. I think it's time for you to deal with your childhood trauma. I know a place in Pennsylvania. They can help you with your family of origin issues and your past trauma. And they might offer you a scholarship."

A few days after talking with Roger, I applied to the Caron Foundation as suggested. They accepted my application. I received a scholarship that paid half the cost, but I didn't have enough money to pay for the other half.

I called Roger back and said, "Hi, Roger. I followed your advice and applied to the Caron Foundation. They will pay for half the tuition."

Roger said, "Rob, that's great!"

I responded, "Yeah, but I don't have any money saved up to pay for the other half."

Roger hesitated to answer. I thought he was going to offer to pay the other half for me. But instead, he said, "Maybe it's time to talk with one of your parents."

Just the thought of talking to them made me feel nauseous. "I don't think I can do that," I admitted.

For several days, I contemplated calling my mom. I finally got up enough courage. We planned to meet at her house. I arrived at my mom's house feeling nervous and reluctant. Like the old days, she had the pressure cooker going, and the hissing sound brought a smile to my face.

"The pinto beans will be done in a few minutes. And I have cornbread in the oven," she said.

"I can't wait. I love your beans and cornbread," I replied.

We sat at the kitchen table, and I stared out the window, watching the birds visiting her bird feeder. I was nervous and fidgeting, picking at my fingernails.

Finally, I looked over at my mom and said, "Mom, my recovery has gone well up to this point. I've been clean and sober for over fourteen years. I'm educated and have a successful teaching career. But I've come to a place in my life where I am emotionally stuck. I have to deal with my childhood trauma."

There was an awkward silence, and my mom looked a bit stunned. Tears welled up in her eyes. I knew she didn't want to talk about the past.

I pushed on.

"We both went through hell together. And I know you, like me, wanted to bury the past and never look back. But I have to deal with it." I paused, took a deep breath, and continued, "Mom, I caused you a lot of pain and watched you almost die, but there is more to it. For almost a year, when you were at work and no one was home, I was raped and sodomized on a regular basis."

My mom let out a shriek, put her head down on the table, and began to cry. She sobbed and sobbed for several minutes. I sat closer to her and said, "I've been holding on to this pain for far too long. It's making me sick. I have to open up so I can let it go. I don't want to cause myself or anyone else more pain."

She stopped crying and wiped her eyes and nose. She caught her breath and said, "Rob, I am so sorry."

I wanted to cry too but had not allowed myself to release any sort of sorrow. I just held onto it and shoved it down. But I did feel my mom's pain and felt her genuine sorrow for all my trauma.

I embraced my mom and confessed with regret, "I never meant to put you through so much pain. I had no idea how to handle the hurt I was going through, so I hurt everyone in my path."

My mom was lost for words. Tears rolled down her face.

I added, "I found an institution that deals with these issues, but I can't afford to pay the cost."

"I'll cover the cost," she offered. My mom and stepdad both had state jobs and were living comfortably.

When I got the call from the Caron Foundation with a bed date, I still had the incision from the second surgery. Again, it was a three-inch surgical wound in the front of my neck.

I had learned a lot in therapy and twelve-step groups about emotions, and I wanted to continue to get better; however, I never wanted to talk about the abuse of my past. While I was scared and I wanted to run away from this entire situation, I knew it was time. All the roadblocks were in place, and I had nowhere to run. I hung up the phone with the Caron Foundation, full of apprehension, and thought, "Over thirty years ago, a man held a knife to my throat and said he'd kill me and my family if I ever told about the abuse. And now I'm going away for five days with this slice in my neck. It is as if I slit my own throat."

I was scared to death walking through those doors. It took every ounce of courage not to run back to my car and go home. My emotional walls were up, determined to keep people at a distance. But by God's grace, I was assigned two perfect counselors: Barbara and Rick.

Barbara greeted me at the door with a warm, welcoming smile. She extended her hand. "Hi, Robert. I'm Barbara. Follow me. I will be doing your intake."

I sat down in her office. Barbara addressed me kindly, saying, "I know you must be very nervous. But don't worry, you are good hands."

I said, "I am definitely nervous."

She asked me the usual intake questions regarding my family history. She wanted to know if I had any brothers and sisters, and who was the oldest and youngest. She asked questions about my mom and dad, their divorce, and how old I was when they separated. She asked about trauma and abuse, and the specific nature.

After the last question, she looked up at me and asked, "Robert, is there something I missed or something you want to add?"

"No, I think you covered all the specifics."

"Good," she said. "I have two more questions for you. What brings you here, and what are you hoping to accomplish?"

I stared at the floor for a few seconds, flipping my thumbs over and over, thinking about my answer. Looking Barbara in the eye, I stopped fidgeting and said, "I was abused as a young boy. I am here to deal with that pain. I want to be able to trust people and to trust God."

My intake goals were complete.

Based on the answers to my intake questions and the brief conversation I had with Barbara, she recommended that I write a letter to my parents using the opposite hand I write with and read it out loud to the group. She explained to me that using my opposite writing hand would assist me with getting in touch with the true emotions I had towards my parents. I wrote the letter and, standing behind an empty chair, read it as if my parents were sitting there. My hands were shaking, and my heart was racing. I wanted to cry, but I did not dare.

After reading the letter, I stood there, looking around the room. My letter expressed my childhood pain and what

I needed and wanted from my parents. There was an awkward silence. I felt exposed and weak. I was on the verge of breaking down but held back the tears with everything I had. Barbara thanked me for my work. The group applauded.

The next assignment was more challenging. I had to figuratively confront the person who had abused me thirty years ago. I met with Barbara and told her that I could not do it.

She responded, "I think we would both agree that the reason you came down here was to do this work."

I nodded in agreement. "I have a strong, overwhelming compulsion to get high. I feel like I want to jump in my car and leave. I'm not sure I can do this work."

Barbara looked into my eyes and said, "Robert, it's time to let go. You can do this."

I cautiously whispered, "I'm scared. I never once thought about the man who abused me. I dismissed the entire situation. I convinced myself that it never happened."

"I know you are, but I know you can do this. If you do decide to leave, please let someone know."

Half an hour before I was to do my assignment, I stopped at the chapel to pray. While I was praying, the maintenance man came in and put a broken vacuum on top of the altar. It disturbed me and made me angry.

I wanted to confront the guy and say, "How can you put a broken vacuum on the altar? You are disrespecting God!"

But then God blessed me with an insight. A quiet peace came over me for a few seconds. I heard God's voice say, "Rob, you are like the broken vacuum, but you can be fixed. I want brokenness to come to the altar. Let Me help you."

My time came. Everyone did their assignment in front of the group until no one was left but me. Rick, my other counselor, assisted with the activity. Rick and I met briefly during my intake. He had a warm, comforting energy. He explained to me that he got into the area of family counseling because of his own childhood trauma.

He said, "Rob, I didn't make mistakes; I was a mistake."

I identified with that statement. It was the story of my life. Although I was scared and unsure, I knew in my heart that I was in the right place. I also knew that Rick and Barbara were the perfect counselors for me.

I stood up and walked toward the empty chair.

Rick handed me a towel and said, "Rob, just keep wringing the towel as if to wring out water."

I took the towel and immediately began wringing it. I had never experienced this kind of fear.

Barbara began, "The person who abused you is sitting in the chair. What do you need to tell him?"

The towel cinched tighter and tighter. I don't know how it didn't rip. I stood there in complete silence, frozen, with a towel wrung as tight as it could get. I had blocked that man out for over thirty years, and now I was standing in front of a group of strangers about to "confront" him. Tears welled up in my eyes.

Rick came up from behind, put his hand on my shoulder, and said, "Robert, it was not your fault."

I collapsed and screamed. Thirty years' worth of tears and pain came out in a flood. For over five minutes, I lay there in a fetal position, sobbing uncontrollably. Barbara rubbed my head and slipped the towel out of my hands. She allowed me to cry until I finally came to a stop.

She whispered in my ear, "Great work, Robert. You have finally begun the process of letting go."

I left Caron Foundation an open wound, figuratively and literally. I still had the long incision in my neck from the surgery, and now my trauma was open and exposed too. Instead of feeling free and excited about moving on with my life, I completely shut down. I went into "safe" mode. My hope was to do the work, be done with it, and move on. But it was not that easy. In fact, things got worse.

I still blocked everyone out of my life and shut down emotionally. To make matters worse, my girlfriend found an article and a picture online of the man who had abused me and shared it with me. The article said he was in prison and would be there for a long time. My girlfriend thought I'd be happy about that. She showed me his picture. I hadn't seen that face in over thirty years. Now, there he was, staring at me through the computer screen. I froze. Within me, everything went completely dark. I wanted to run and hide again. I wanted to crawl into a hole and die, the same way I felt so many years ago as a little boy.

My first instinct was to jump on my bike and go for a long ride. But that escape route was gone. I was too overweight, too out of shape, and still recovering from surgery. The pain inside became overwhelming, and I didn't see a way out. I planned another suicide. Here I was, fourteen years sober, writing a letter to my girlfriend: "I can't take the pain anymore. I don't see a way out."

I jumped in my car and decided I would drown myself in Willowemoc Creek. I drove down my road. It was the eeriest feeling, as if everything was in slow motion, dreamlike. I didn't want to die, but I didn't see a way out. I didn't want to talk about it; I just wanted the pain to go away. Coming to the end of the road, I looked straight ahead. On an old barn, a yellow road sign said, "Dead End Cafe," with an arrow pointing to the right. I was struck with the thought, "Dead end. This can't be the end."

Suddenly, I decided that I would not jump into the river. Instead, I drove to a state park where I used to hike and decided to put a hose in my car's exhaust and snake it through the back window. When I arrived at the park, ready to implement my plan, I couldn't do it. Realizing I needed help, I drove to the local hospital that had a mental health ward. Pausing in the parking lot, I tried to conjure up the courage to check myself in. Within minutes, I heard a tapping on my window.

A state police officer stood there, tapping with his nightstick. He asked, "Are you Robert Woods?"

I nodded my head. "Yes."

He said, "Please put your hands on the steering wheel."

I complied.

He asked, "Are there any weapons in the car?"

I shook my head. "No."

In a professional and understanding voice, he instructed, "I'm going to open the door. I want you to leave your hands on the steering wheel. Is that understood?"

I nodded my head.

He opened the door and placed a handcuff on one of my wrists. "I need you to step out of the car."

I stepped out.

"Put your hands behind your back." As soon as I did, he handcuffed my arms behind my back and walked me into the hospital. I never understood why I was handcuffed. I guess it's protocol for officers dealing with people who want to harm themselves.

"Rob, you have to say something," my sister pleaded.

I was sitting on a bench in the general area of the emergency room. There were medical professionals attending multiple situations. It was chaos. My sister sat beside me, rubbing my back and shoulders. When my girlfriend read my suicide letter, she called the state police and then my sister. My sister arrived at the hospital about an hour after I got there. I sat there, handcuffed and mute. I could hear everything going on around me, but I could not speak a word. I wanted to, but I was completely frozen. Maya Angelou once wrote about being mute after her trauma, too.

The state police officer who'd brought me into the hospital stood five feet away, talking with another local police officer.

The local police officer looked at me and then said to the state police officer, "The mind is a terrible thing to waste."

I wanted to jump up and punch him in his face. But I had no fight left. I just sat there, frozen. No one knew what was going on. They didn't know my trauma and that I had seen a picture of the person who had abused me. They didn't know anything. No one did. Except my sponsor and my mother.

My sister sat next to me and continued to press, "Rob, talk to me. What's the matter?"

But I sat there, staring at the floor, mute, like May Angelou did several weeks after she was raped. She wrote, "I walked into rooms where people were laughing, their voices hitting the walls like stones, and I simply stood still—in the midst of the riot of sound."

She pleaded again, "Rob, they are not going to let you out of here if you don't talk. Tell me what's the matter."

There were no words. My sister and I sat for more than

twelve hours until I was moved to a mental institution via ambulance.

Although the hospital was a horrifying place, I'm grateful I didn't follow through with the suicide. Once admitted, I shared a room with a person who suffered from Turret Syndrome. He would look at me and say, "F*ck you," and then he would check his watch, over and over. The windows were fitted with steel mesh screens, making it impossible to get out. We were in a locked ward. The only way in or out was through locked doors with security officers posted by the doors. I was a caged animal.

On my first day in the ward, I left my room to use the bathroom and noticed one of the patients showing another patient how to walk using her arms. I heard her say, "If you don't swing your arms when you walk, they will never let you out of here."

I noticed a different patient, who wore a hospital gown and never took it off, doing laps around the nurse's station, mumbling incoherently. Before I got close to the bathroom, two security guards ran around the corner and restrained a patient. I stared at the incident and thought, "I really don't belong here."

I completely shut down. I refused to participate in any group work, or any activity scheduled for the day. One day, I wanted to call home. I walked up to the nurses' station and said, "I need to make a phone call."

The nurse said, "You can only make phone calls between four and five."

I argued, "Well, I'm making a phone call now."

I walked over to the phone and proceeded to dial. She

called security, and two security officers ran up and asked, "What are you doing?"

"I'm making a phone call," I told them.

One of them said, "No, you're not. You can make a phone call during phone call hours."

I felt like I was gonna come out of my skin. I roared back, "What the hell are you gonna do?"

He chuckled and said, "We don't have to go down this path. Hang up the phone and use it during phone hours."

I said nothing and put the phone down and walked away. I went into my room and sat on top of the nightstand, refusing to use a chair. It was a total rebellion mode for me. If they said sit, I would stand. If they said lights out, I would leave the light on. My behavior was that of an uncivilized human being. I thought about animals I had seen in zoos aggressively pacing back and forth in their cages. I felt like that. I looked out my window, gazing down on the trees.

Feeling emotionally destitute, I sat there on that nightstand. Still upset about not being able to use the phone, I wondered how the hell I wound up in this horrible place. I thought about my studies and how I was over a year into my doctorate program. I thought about how far I'd come and how much I had turned my life around. But now I felt all alone and confused. Without explanation, sitting on the nightstand, I heard God's voice.

He said, "You don't belong in a cage, but the man who abused you does. You need to forgive him to let go of the pain."

In that moment, a peace beyond understanding came over me. Everything inside of me changed. My confusion cleared. My anger dissipated. I no longer felt alone.

I said, out loud, "God, I do forgive him. I don't hate him. I feel sad for him."

From that moment on, I was freed from the trauma of my past. God unlocked the prison I had locked myself in so many years ago. I finally let go and let God.

The portable Velodrome. Just before I had to stop riding because of herniated cervical discs.

CHAPTER THIRTEEN

From Prison to Prison

"As I walked out the door toward the gate that would lead to my freedom, I knew if I didn't leave my bitterness and hatred behind, I'd still be in prison."

- Nelson Mandela

When I left the mental institution a changed person, I was lighter; I did not feel weighed down by the burdens of my past. Maya Angelou wrote, "The caged bird sings because he has a song to sing." God opened the door to the emotional prison that held me captive for thirty years. All this time, the long-sought-after key was forgiveness. I had to reach the point of no return before I was able to choose forgiveness. I do not recommend this path. Pray to forgive. Pray for the person. Talk to others you trust. Forgiveness will come. And when it does, you will be free, too. Forgiveness does not absolve the abuser of their crime; it sets you free from their power over you.

In a matter of months, after leaving the mental hospital, my whole world changed. It was time for me to clear the toxicity from my life. An unhealthy romantic relationship I was holding onto with my girlfriend had to end. We got into a spat a few days after my return home. After the argument, I explained with confidence that we needed to call it quits.

Ending that relationship was a welcome relief. It was empowering and freeing. Next, I had to let go of my entry-level career job. I had left the Catholic school teaching job to teach in a public school. Two years into that position, due to budget cuts, I was let go. I accepted a job at the local alcohol and rehabilitation center. A friend suggested I apply for a job teaching in prison. I did. Within a month, I was offered a job to teach for the Department of Corrections.

I was a confident teacher with classroom management skills and a knack for handling negative situations. Despite all the changes and recent personal growth, when I walked into my classroom at the prison, I felt like a first-year teacher almost identical to my first day teaching sixth grade. One by one, men entered my classroom wearing green uniforms stamped with their DIN numbers. The DIN number is a number assigned to an incarcerated individual upon reception into a correctional facility. This number is used throughout an incarcerated individual's term of commitment. I chose not to refer to the men by their numbers. Instead, I addressed them in the manner that they preferred, first name or last name.

On my first day, I introduced myself. "Hi, everyone. I'm Mr. Woods. I'll be preparing you for the high school equivalency test." Most of the men slouched in their chairs and gave me a cold stare, saying nothing. I said with a smile on my face, "Okay. Cool. Glad you are all happy to be here."

I got a few chuckles and began my first lesson.

As a teacher and a reading specialist, I knew the importance of good reading skills. Every afternoon, I would read aloud to them. Half of the class cringed and resisted.

One particular inmate, a notorious gang member, took a strong posture in front of me, complaining, "Yo, Mr. Woods, can you not read to us? I feel like an asshole sitting here."

With a confident smile, I replied, "I want to model what good reading sounds like for you guys. It's important for your brains to hear and absorb good reading."

He raised his voice. "I don't care. All my friends can see me when they walk by our classroom."

"My intent is not to make you feel like an asshole. I really want you to hear and absorb good reading habits," I assured him.

He continued to complain and got some of the other inmates to complain, too.

One afternoon, I decided to cancel my afternoon reading and do individual lessons instead. My loudest complainer shouted out in a friendly way, "Yo, Mr. Woods, why you ain't reading out loud to us? I kind of like it now."

It felt like a hug, and I smiled. "Sure. I'd be glad to."

I identified with the men's situation. I knew their lives presented them with some serious challenges, and going to school seemed unimportant. Trust and relationships take time, and I understood that. I had been in situations like that before. I never pushed and always conveyed concern for their future. Over time, the men realized I genuinely cared for them. The magic and beauty of teaching began in a prison for me. I respected the men, and they respected me.

I took a special interest in one individual. He always talked to me after class. He really wanted to learn.

"With hard work and practice, you'll learn and pass the GED test, no problem," I assured him.

He had a glow in his eye. "You really think I can?"

"Absolutely, and remember, for every hour in the classroom, it's three hours of practice on your own."

I think he didn't want me to get the wrong impression of him. One day, he explained, "You know, Mr. Woods, I'm not a bad guy. But my neighborhood is rough. A drug dealer slapped my sister. I confronted him, and he pulled a gun on me. I had to shoot him. It was self-defense. I got sentenced to ten years."

I thanked him for sharing with me and said, "Well, take advantage of the opportunities afforded to you while incarcerated."

With a sheepish voice, he mumbled, "Yo, I was always in special classes in school. I hated school and hated those classes. But I like your class. Can you teach me how to write?"

Beaming with delight, I said, "Absolutely."

We worked together for several weeks on an essay, and the result was a well-written essay that was his, not mine.

When we finished, with a big smile on his face, he praised me, "Yo, Mr. Woods. You're a good teacher. I never had a teacher get to my 'knot' like you." He was referring to his mind, his way of thinking. Because of my background, I knew how to communicate with him and the other men. It was then that I knew: I was called to teach in prison.

I accepted a promotion within the correctional system to be the Director of Education at a maximum-security prison. I would be responsible for supervising the academic and vocational programs, the library, the recreation department, and the college programs. In addition, I was a tier three hearing officer which is someone who decides whether an inmate is innocent or guilty of a ticket they received from correctional officers.

My new boss declared, "Mr. Woods, I don't care how you do it, but you need to manage these teachers. They need direction."

Unbeknownst to me, the Education Department had not had an immediate supervisor for several months. It was a rudderless ship.

Looking my boss in the eye, I replied, "Okay, I'll do my best."

It was by far the most challenging but, more importantly, the most rewarding job I've ever had. My first day as Director of Education was a no-contact day for students. Students were given the day off so teachers could spend the day in preparation for the upcoming school year. That morning, I started the day by holding my first faculty meeting.

I introduced myself and told the group, "I have an activity. Take fifteen minutes to think of the educator who had the most impact on you. And then, we will share it. No one is required to share if they don't want to."

I did the activity, too. I shared first.

With an enthusiastic voice, I said, "My assistant principal during seventh grade had the most influence on me. I was always in his office, but he always took the time to ask me how I was and if I was okay. I have never forgotten him."

A few of the teachers shared positively. One teacher

shared something that will stay with me forever. He said almost angrily, "I got one. My music teacher. Every time I missed a note, he screamed at me. I hated him and hated music. I never took another music class."

His response stunned me. Uncomfortable and a little embarrassed, I said, "I wasn't prepared for that response. It caught me off guard. But it coincides with my message to all of you. Remember, always think about what is best for your students, not what is best for you."

Overall, my first faculty meeting went well. It was a great kick-off. The teachers gained some insight of me and my leadership style. Likewise, I opened a window to understand them and their personalities.

Soon after I settled in, I visited the religious services across the hall. I wanted to meet the Catholic priest and see the chapel. I entered the priest's office. On the back wall was a mural of a local area I liked to hike near Lake Awosting. There were shelves of Catholic books, a closet for the priest's clothing, and a desk. When I arrived, two inmates were sitting in there, his clerks.

His head clerk jumped up and shook my hand. He was genuinely happy to see me. With a big smile, he said, "Welcome aboard."

"Thank you. I'm glad to be here," I replied.

The inmate looked at me and then over at the priest and said, "Don't listen to this idiot."

We both laughed. The priest stood up and introduced himself as Father Stan. Father Stan stood about five feet, three inches, but had the confidence of a giant. He spoke with his native Eastern Nigerian accent.

I shook his hand and said, "Nice to meet you. I'm

Robert Woods." At the time, I had no idea that Father Stan would become my mentor and best friend.

I spent a lot of time in Father's office. He possessed a PhD in psychology and understood human development well. He once told me, "Robert, the problem with Americans is they cannot handle the plain truth."

Laughing, I responded, "Father, please give me the plain truth, even when I don't want to hear it."

And he always has. He mentored my emotional well-being by telling me things I didn't want to hear but needed to hear. He grew my spiritual fitness by praying for me and giving me sound spiritual direction. He mentored me through my doctoral process because he had experience completing a doctoral program and knew how to write a dissertation. When I thought things were too difficult, he would say, "Shut up, Robert. Kill the beast!"

One day in his office, I had a profound experience. Father had clearly defined relationships with the inmates. They either loved him or hated him; there were no grey areas with Father Stan. One of the inmates who loved him, a prominent gang member, came into his office and asked, "Why are you always pushing up on me?"

Father looked at him with a mope look on his face, one he taught me to master, and said, "Shut up, idiot." Father explained that when dealing with aggressive people, give them a dumb look rather than argue.

I sat there in awe. A priest normally would not speak in this manner. But he has a way with people where it just works.

The inmate looked at him, shaking his head, and said, "You're a trip." The chemistry between them was special.

It was a true father-son relationship. I felt so blessed to be able to witness that. This inmate had so much love and respect for Father that his hard gang presence would melt away. It was witnessing that moment that my dissertation question was born: "What do prison educators perceive to be their role in the transformative experiences of inmates?" My epiphany was that it's not the programs that transform people; it's the people who implement them.

Although my passion for the subject was always present, it was a laborious process to finish my dissertation. I was easily distracted. Father Stan would continuously remind me by saying, "Robert, kill the beast." He knew the dissertation process was stressful. He made sure I didn't become an ABD doctoral student, all but dissertation. Every time I made an edit, my dissertation would have to go to my dissertation chair and then to two other members of my committee. It would then return to me with double the number of suggested edits.

At one point, I was struggling with Chapter Two, a review of the literature. I had been working on it for months when my dissertation chair suggested I take a leave of absence because it was taking so long.

I handed Father Stan two months of work on Chapter Two, and he shook his head and shrugged his shoulders. "Robert, throw it out. It's trash."

I couldn't believe he said to throw it out. I was so proud of it. With a dejected expression, I shrugged my shoulders, and admitted, "I don't know what to do."

Father advised, "Robert, find some completed dissertations and read their chapter twos."

My eyes teared up. "Okay, Father Stan, I will read other dissertations."

Finding award-winning dissertations, I printed their second chapters. I even slept with them under my pillow. Finally, the solution dawned on me: I did not need to give an opinion on the research as I had been doing. That was for Chapter Five. I needed only to explain what each researcher's study presented, not whether I agreed with it or not. I then completed Chapter Two in less than three weeks.

Successfully defending my dissertation, I officially became Dr. Robert Woods in 2010. The dedication read:

This dissertation is dedicated to my father, Joe Don Woods, whose life transformation transformed my own life and led me to do this research. My father's transformation guided me out of a world of pain and destruction into a world of personal growth, opportunity, and self-love. His strength taught me the value of persistence, which allowed me to continue my research when so many times I wanted to quit. My father's love allowed me to experience a full life when I was headed for a life filled with emptiness. Thank you, Dad, for being you.

Father Stan and Dr. Keen, my dissertation chair, often told me, "You can't give a speech without a platform. Finish up your schoolwork!"

So, I did. I now had a platform with life experience and academics to support it. My platform was to use my education, passion, and gifts to help and encourage troubled souls.

As a director of education in a maximum-security prison, I frequently had problem students in my office. Their teachers always said, "I don't know what you say to them, but they always come back to class with a different mindset." It was never about what I said. It was about identifying with their reality. Considering my life and what I've been through, I could certainly do that.

One day, the head cook stopped me in the hallway and said, "Dr. Woods, when you go into the yard, it's like watching Moses parting the Red Sea. The men cut a path for you. They love you."

That meant a lot to me because, sometimes, it felt like I wasn't making a difference. His recognition was an affirmation that, actually, I was. I am forever grateful that God unlocked the door to my mental prison and, ironically, placed me in a maximum-security prison so I could help men like me, caught up in life's hardships. I transitioned from hating school as a teen to spending my entire professional career motivating unwilling students to appreciate the value of learning.

CHAPTER FOURTEEN

A Badge of Honor

"Most people never run far enough on their first wind to find out they've got a second."

- William James

When I left the institution after my suicide attempt, I weighed almost three hundred pounds. Because of my vertebral surgeries, I had stopped exercising and gained a lot of weight. Instead of talking about my feelings and practicing the recovery principles I had learned, I became addicted to food, specifically sugar. Sugar triggers dopamine in a similar way that drugs do. I knew the pounds were coming on, but the depression had zapped me of motivation. My situation felt hopeless, and I feared that it would not get better. I had no idea the hatred and toxic shame had been holding me down. However, now that I was free of that toxicity, I slowly began to exercise again. Forgiveness was my first step in the process toward wellness. Now I was working on motivation, confidence, and self-worth.

Within a month of leaving the mental hospital, I began

cutting ties with unhealthy relationships and developed a healthier relationship with myself.

One day, at a friend's house, I noticed pictures on the wall of him finishing marathons at different locations. I exclaimed, "Wow, that's great. I can't believe you ran five marathons!"

He handed me a yellow book, *The Runners Handbook*, and said, "You can, too."

When I began training for my first marathon, I weighed almost three hundred pounds and could not run more than half a mile. After two weeks, I developed shin splints and could hardly walk. In addition, I had two fused discs in my cervical spine and had to be careful not to overdo it. I could not see how anyone enjoyed running. Even though it was the most uncomfortable form of exercise I had ever participated in, I ran anyway. Rather than focusing on the physical challenges, I focused on how good I felt mentally after each run. Those runs, for me, were endorphin-inducing and helped me to think more clearly. I guess it's what people call a *runner's high*.

My aches and pains lessened with each week of continued training, and my overall sense of well-being improved. Five months after my friend handed me the book, on May 25, 2008, I ran my first marathon in Burlington, Vermont. I gave my finisher medal to my mom. With a grateful smile, I rejoicingly told her, "Mom, I'm giving you my medal. You ran your own marathon chasing after me all those years."

Life continued to improve. Three months later, I returned from attending my last residency for my doctoral program. Upon arriving, my friend Ron called me to say, "Rob, Kristen from our twelve-step meeting is considering entering a doctoral program and wanted to talk to you about it. Are you available?"

"Yeah, I can help her," I replied, "I'll give her a call."

I called Kristen and said, "Hey, I heard you had some questions about getting a doctorate. Did you want to talk?"

With measured concern in her voice, she said, "Yes, but right now, I am looking for my dog. He ran away."

"I'm sorry to hear that," I said. "I can come and help you look for him."

With reluctance, she replied, "Okay. But I am an emotional mess right now."

We spent the day looking for him but never found him. Physically and emotionally exhausted from the search, we took a break at a local café. Though it was heartbreaking for Kristen to lose her dog (we never found him), in those moments we knew that it was love at "hello."

Kristen asked, "Have you ever read Richard Bach?"

I regarded her with a quizzical look on my face and said, "That's my line. Richard Bach is my favorite author."

We both laughed about the coincidence. Richard Bach is one of her favorite authors, too. We shared many favorites, including *Jonathan Livingston Seagull*, *Illusions*, and *The Bridge Across Forever*. They are biographical in nature with fictional characters. He is adept at diving into human nature while illustrating philosophical and metaphysical insights. Kristen even wrote to him once, asking for advice about writing. The band Deep Blue Something had "Breakfast at Tiffany's." Kristen and I had Richard Bach.

We knew we were perfect for one another. That summer went by with shared meals, movies, hikes, and lots of trail running. We told each other our hopes, dreams, thoughts, and opinions about life and living. Eventually, the subject of marriage came up. While running together at one of our favorite spots, Walnut Mountain, we stopped at the lookout like we always did, to enjoy the view. I got down on one knee and asked her to marry me.

Two months later, on October 9, 2008, we eloped in the town of Lake Placid, NY, a place we both love dearly. We agreed to elope because we had both already done the traditional wedding and were divorced. Standing on the lawn by the shore of Mirror Lake (the lake in the center of town), the Adirondack mountains guarded the horizon while the sun blessed us with its full glory on that unusually warm October morning. Looking over the lake with the mountains in the distance, and the town behind us, it was the idyllic space in which we wanted to exchange our vows and begin our married life together. While the justice of the peace read our vows, we saw only each other. His wife attended as our witness. We invited no one else.

When we finished the ceremony, he said, "You may now kiss the bride."

We kissed and immediately heard exuberant and uproarious applause and cheering. As we looked around, we saw that every space to sit or stand in the park was occupied by onlookers watching us get married. It seemed like the entire town was there just for us. We cried tears of joy. Ten months later, Kristen gave birth to our beautiful daughter. We named her Hope for all of the ways she represented that for us.

Even though I was now married with an infant daughter and still working on my doctorate, I continued to run marathons. After completing the Hartford Marathon for the second time, a thought struck me: *I would like to use my running to inspire others.* I knew training helped me reduce stress, and I felt good when I successfully completed an event. But something was missing. My training needed a purpose.

I began praying for purpose. Soon after, my younger brother, JoÚ, called me. "Rob, I'm putting together a not-for-profit organization called Upright Africa. I'm looking for ways to promote my efforts to help the people of the Congo. Are you interested?" he asked.

I eagerly replied, "Absolutely. I've been praying for God to show me how to use my running to help others. And you called."

His reply echoed my thoughts. "God must have a plan."

It wasn't until I saw a performance called "Vagina Monologues" that I became spiritually connected to using my training and my past to help others. One day, Kristen asked me if I wanted to go with her to see it at a local college.

I said, "Sure, I'll go," never anticipating the play's impact.

"It's a powerful message about rape and might present challenges for you," Kristen warned.

I honestly didn't give it much thought. Kristen was excited about it and had seen it before during her undergraduate work in Colorado. Being in a good place both mentally and spiritually, without hesitation, I agreed.

The most powerful scene, for me, was the village scene. Eve Ensler, the playwright, quoted a Bosnian woman who compared her sexuality to a village. After being raped repeatedly as a tactic of war, the woman said, "I do not touch now. I do not visit. I live someplace else now. I don't know where that is."

I identified with this woman. I knew how she felt. I felt a flood of emotions during that scene. It immediately brought me back to my childhood days, reminding me of the years' worth of rapes and the agony of not telling anyone.

Drifting back in time, I recalled the darkness. I remembered the feeling of shame as though I was covered in dirt and filth and how badly I wanted it off me. Washing myself over and over again, I remember how I tried to cleanse myself, but I still felt dirty. How I wanted my mother and father to hold me and take me back to the way things had been; things like sitting at the top of the stairs with my brothers and sister on Christmas mornings, waiting to see what Santa Claus brought or just a simple dinner together in the dining room. That one scene made me revisit my trauma and recall how, every day, I had wanted to crawl into a hole and die.

Bringing me back from my spiraling thoughts, Kristen nudged me and whispered, "Rob, are you alright?"

I snapped out of my stupor and came back to the present. "Yes, I'm okay." And for a moment, I felt sad for my younger self who had endured so much pain. It was after that scene that I knew I had a responsibility to help others who had been traumatized by sexual abuse.

In 2011, I felt prompted by God to run an ultramarathon. JoÚ and I continuously talked about ways I could promote Upright Africa. We decided to make shirts with the organization's logo and the inscription, "I Can Do All Things Through Christ Who Strengthens Me." Only we hadn't decided on a race yet. For some unexplained reason, I thought about the time my older brother Ben, his middle son, and I visited the Palo Duro Canyon. We learned about the endurance run they host while we were there, but I had not become an ultra-runner yet. I didn't think much about the race then, but now here it was. I called Ben and told him how excited I was to run this race, especially since we were there not too long ago. I told him it would be a great opportunity to heal some of the wounds from our broken past and to promote JoÚ's organization.

The run opened the door for Ben and me to have long conversations regarding our childhood, specifically the abuse I endured and his role at that time. I told him about some of the details leading to my mental breakdown. He apologized for not visiting me while I was in the hospital. With frustration and anger in his voice, he said, "I called Dad and screamed at him. I told him to get you the hell out of that place." The Palo Duro Endurance Run provided the opportunity for us to talk in depth about the darkness of our past.

Palo Duro turned out to be a spiritual and healing process. It took everyone's (my father, son, brothers and sister, uncle and aunt, nieces, nephews, and friends) effort for me to complete the fifty miles in the one-hundred-five-degree heat. Kristen stayed home to care for Hope, who was too young to be outside in the heat for twelve hours waiting for me to finish.

It felt like God was in charge that day. When the gun sounded at 5 a.m. and the runners took off in the darkness of the canyon, a few hundred feet down the trail, a man in his Celtic skirt stood playing the bagpipes. It sent chills down my spine. It was a great send-off. My support crew gelled together. Everyone knew what to do and was more than willing to offer support; no one person was in charge. There was a natural order to the day.

The race director allowed most of my support crew to run with me for the last few miles of the race. It was a magical experience. The run confirmed that I was not running from myself but running to God and for His glory. I came to realize that endurance sports can serve as a promoter for personal growth and transformation. The Palo Duro Trail Run paved the way for my path to endurance, my connection with God, and the ability to show people that you can follow your dreams after being traumatized and abused.

After completing the Palo Duro run, I wanted to test my limits again and was inspired to run a hundred-miler, also known as a "century." On July 19, 2014, I scheduled my first hundred-mile ultramarathon, the Vermont 100. At the start line, I set up a tent the night before the race. The thoughts I encountered while lying in that tent took me back to my early childhood days when I was first abused. I remembered building a wall around my heart so nobody would ever hurt me again and using drugs and alcohol to numb my pain and hide from those feelings. The fear was paralyzing, and I felt unable to take risks. In my tent, I momentarily allowed an overpowering negative voice (the lunatic) to take control. It began: *"Why are you doing this? You're going to fail. Maybe all those people who have been telling you that running one hundred miles is insane and not healthy were right."*

I tried to shut down the negative assault, but it kept

coming. *"Who do you think you are, trying to do something like this? You're not good enough."*

Suddenly, a voice outside startled me back to the present, "Can you guys please settle down? It's after ten o'clock."

The voices of the other runners brought me back to reality, and I laughed out loud and whispered to myself, "I'm not alone. And I can do this."

I was definitely not alone. There were over three hundred other runners who would embark upon the same one-hundred-mile challenge the next morning. My family was there to support me. My younger brother, JoÚ, would pace me at mile seventy. I thought of all the training and preparation I had done for this event. I told that lousy voice that it would no longer control me and said to myself, "I *am* worthy, and this run *will* provide hope to many others who need it. I *must* do this run. I can no longer be afraid to take risks."

I was reminded of another runner's comment: "No pain, no summit." The journey would be painful, and I knew it. But the joy would be in the journey.

Kristen and her best friend, Carolyn, drove me to the start line the night before. As I was leaving, my family and friends surrounded me in a circle. Each one in attendance placed a hand on my body, and my dad shared some words of wisdom. My stepdad, Deacon Don, closed the experience with a prayer of triumph. It was such a wonderful feeling to have everyone laying hands on me. It gave me the strength I needed to embark on a one-hundred-mile run. I got goosebumps and that tingling, champagne-like sensation—the feeling my younger, traumatized self chased with drugs and alcohol. This time, I had that through self-healing, self-care, and self-improvement. I have since labeled that experience as "God hugs."

For so many years, I did things alone. I did not want help, especially from family. My motto was, "Stay away from me." For me, it was beautiful to be able to share an extraordinary event with the people I love and open my heart to them. I encourage anyone reading this book not to shut down. Be open to love from others because it's love that heals.

Three hundred runners and I began the run in the 4 a.m. darkness. I listened to the conversations around me. As I ran through the woods with them, my overpowering negative voice disappeared, and I was at peace. I ran the first forty-seven miles with no problems aside from the usual upset stomach. Feeling strong and encouraged, I cruised into the mile forty-seven aid station. My entire support crew was waiting: my wife, dad, sister, stepmom, brother, uncle, and niece. I had to weigh in, and I was only down four pounds. Medical personnel reminded me to keep eating and to watch my hydration. My brother ran up to me and said, "You're looking good for mile thirty-one!"

"Mile thirty-one? This is mile forty-seven!" I exclaimed. I felt amazing and thought I would easily complete the race in under twenty-four hours.

With a surprised look, he raised his hand for a high five and shouted, "Damn bro, you're killing it!"

I asked my sister for my second set of sneakers, and she had the "deer in headlights" look. I asked, confused, "This is a handler station. How come you can't give me my shoes?"

My sister realized the mistake and said, "I don't have your bags, they're back at the camp."

I felt a little disappointed about not having fresh sneakers, but I was not upset. Everyone was giving me so much love and support, I couldn't have asked for anything more. I also knew that these things happen at endurance events. The key was to use them for fuel and not get bogged down by negative emotions.

My team met with the aid station director, who informed us that the next handler station was twelve miles away. Shuffling out of the aid station, I kept going. My stomach was queasy, and it was hard to hold down food. I kept moving and smiled to myself. My crew assured me that they would see me in twelve miles.

As I ran, I thought about my team and how they were handling the mistake. It made me think about how life throws a lot of curveballs, situations that are beyond our control. I used to hold onto anger, resentment, hatred, and shame. Life's curves would feed those negative emotions. Now that I had let go of hatred and resentment, uncontrollable happenings became opportunities for me to grow.

I met my family twelve miles later at mile fifty-nine, and everyone was settled and smiling. Unable to keep my food down, the only thing that sounded good was yogurt. I asked my crew to get me some yogurt for the next aid station. In the meantime, I managed to eat some crackers.

My niece, Casey, said, "Uncle Rob, do you want an ice-cold Dr. Pepper?"

My face lit up at the suggestion. I smiled approvingly, "Casey, you're a lifesaver. Thank you!" I sucked down half of it, and with that, I was almost ready to move on.

A change out of sweat-soaked sneakers and socks provided much-needed relief. Fresh socks and sneakers are gifts from heaven during an endurance race.

As I changed, my dad said to me, "Son, you're looking better and better at each aid station." I could tell by his expression that he knew my odds of completing the run were good.

We made eye contact, smiled, and I said, "Thanks, Dad. I'll see you at the next aid station."

My dad and I have been on our own lifelong journey together. After I left the aid station, I could feel my dad's relief and used it for motivation to keep going. For many years, I was so angry at my parents for not protecting me. As I ran, I reflected, knowing deep down that no matter what happened throughout my life, my mom and dad truly loved me and always have. They were fighting their own demons, too.

My stomach continued to plague me, and I knew I needed calories. When I arrived at aid station sixty-five, a man asked, "Would you like a hamburger or a hot dog?"

I perked up. "A hot dog would be great." I ate the hot dog with mustard. That did the trick! My stomach was back to somewhat normal. I thought to myself, "Relief comes in unexpected ways. Who would have thought a hot dog would settle my stomach?"

The simple, unexpected relief of eating that hot dog caused me to reflect. So many times, throughout my life, help was sent to me in ways that I'd least expected. In most cases, I was resistant. But sometimes, the struggle to keep a wall up became too difficult, and its breakdown was inevitable. Eventually, I realized that help is out there if you're open to receiving it. Accept it, don't reject it.

I made it to mile seventy feeling strong and confident. I got to my brother, JoÚ, before dark. It was 8:15 p.m. JoÚ would pace me and support me physically and emotionally for the next thirty miles. I told JoÚ before the run that, if I made it to him, he had to promise me he would not let me quit. Wow! What a thirty-mile journey we experienced.

Coming into the mile seventy aid station, I was greeted by so many: my son, daughter-in-law, and grandchildren were new additions, and it was great to see them all. My sister handed me a cup of yogurt and a yogurt smoothie. I could sense her feeling of redemption regarding the sneaker mishap. Her genuine love for me was obvious. The food provided me with the necessary relief for my stomach and calories for my body. My brother was eager to get going, and we set off. As we ran, I pictured my sister's face in my mind.

Thinking of my sister, I reflected on our relationship throughout my life and my journey to wellness. Before I found relief for my abuse and emotional pain, I would get drunk all the time. In the wee hours of the night, I would call my sister just to hear her voice. I would tell her that I wanted to die, but ultimately, what I wanted was to stop hurting. Eight years prior to this run, my sister sat with me for hours at the hospital when I wanted to end it all with suicide. As I ran, I thought about how awesome it was that everyone knew about my abuse. I didn't have to hide secrets anymore. My sister was there providing support to me now that I was open to receiving it.

JoÚ and I took a turn into the woods. It was getting dark, and we began an ascent that seemed to never end. I was still feeling good, but nightfall was bringing drowsiness. Slowly, the pep in my step began to fade. By the time we reached the next aid station, mile seventy-seven, my wheels seemed like they had all fallen off. I was so tired. My confidence wavered, and I started to doubt that I would finish. This seemed like a replay of my life. Whenever things seemed to get better, the negative voice would say, "It won't last. You don't deserve to feel good about anything." Man, I hate that voice. But here it was in my head again. Thank God for my brother JoÚ! He was a gift of light out there in the dark.

I believe God sends life-gifts in the form of people; be willing to accept them. It is so hard to trust after being abused. It feels safer not to trust. However, once you get past the overpowering negative voices and emotions, trust your God-given instincts and those who love you; they will always provide guidance and support, much like JoÚ did to get me to the finish line.

I think mile eighty-three was the most challenging. It had to be around 4 a.m. (twenty-four hours since the race's start), and all I wanted was sleep. My butt was chaffed so badly that I had to hold one of my cheeks to keep them from rubbing together. There are medicines and aids to help with chaffing, but I was so new to the sport, I didn't know about them. It was excruciating. My right ankle and foot were throbbing, too. My brain began to drift, and I begged my brother to let me sleep against a tree for only ten minutes.

JoÚ replied, "We'll talk about it at the next aid station." It became his mantra for the rest of the race: "We'll talk about it at the next aid station."

There were many nights, before I found wellness, that JoÚ had to carry me home on his shoulder because I was too drunk to walk. I don't know what happened or how, but as I ran with him through mile eighty-three, I went from a state of not knowing how I could take another step to a quiet, gentle peace, knowing that I would finish.

It's so true when people say, "Keep going until the miracle happens." I pray that anyone needing help to overcome trauma and abuse will trust the healing process and not give up before a miracle happens. Lean on someone and put your trust in him or her to guide you to wellness. Trust the process. Trust God. I know it's hard, but it's a metamorphosis worth the experience. There is so much pain and hurt, but in the end, a butterfly is born, a beautiful, untainted soul.

I did not sleep against a tree. JoÚ and I met my crew at mile eighty-eight. Before they even saw us, they knew we were coming because they could hear us laughing as we came out of the woods into the aid station.

Just before we arrived, a runner passed us, and JoÚ said, "Great work. You can do a buck ten."

The runner stopped and said, "What's a buck ten?"

JoÚ replied, "One hundred and ten miles."

The runner looked at us with a twisted face and let out a groan. "No way!"

We laughed so hard.

It was so awesome to see my sister, dad, and stepmom in the wee hours of the night, committed to making sure I finished. It is not an easy process to let people help, but I knew it was necessary for me to heal. There are mean, awful people in the world. But there are also beautiful people with gentle souls willing to love. Don't chase them away.

Leaving mile eighty-eight, my mind quiet and my body in pain, JoÚ and I continued our journey to the finish line. I watched countless runners pass me, and I wanted to go faster, but my chaffed butt and sore ankle prevented it. I continued at a slow, steady pace, coaxing myself to just finish.

A runner passed us in the night and said, "You can't quit now! In a few hours, you got bragging rights!"

JoÚ and I finished together at 8:16 a.m., twenty-eight hours and sixteen minutes after I began. Just under the thirty-hour cut off time. My wife, son, sister, father, stepmother, niece, and uncle all cheered and shared in this incredible moment (Caryolyn was with Hope, still asleep at the campsite). I was glad to be finished, and I will never forget the joyful hugs from everyone after I crossed that line. I will be forever grateful to everyone who supported me.

The day after the run, I could hardly walk, and my right ankle and foot had swollen up like a plum. I had cuts on my feet because I had forgotten to loosen my laces when my feet swelled. My chaffed butt was sore, and I knew it would be days before it would heal. As expected, my entire body ached. I would whine and complain every time I moved, especially going down stairs.

At one point, my wife looked at me and said, "Honey, wear your pain as a badge of honor. You did it. You earned it." She followed with, "Wear the pain from your abuse as a badge of honor, too. You survived."

At first, her words didn't really impact me, but as the hours passed, I realized what she meant. My pain is a badge of honor. I survived the horrendous abuse. I am not the ugly monster that I felt inside for so many years. The person who abused me is the monster. With dignity, I can hold my head high.

CHAPTER FIFTEEN

Back on the Bike

"The bicycle is a curious vehicle. Its passenger is its engine."

- John Howard, US cyclist

Soon after the Vermont 100, I got to thinking that I would like to begin riding my bicycle again. I had trepidation because, in the past, every time I started riding bicycles, I would get too absorbed or get injured. But this time, it felt different. God had freed me from my anger, resentment, and hatred. I was no longer trying to escape from myself or my life. Cycling would no longer be an escape route.

In time, I started to get my cycling legs back. I told a friend at work about my ultramarathons and how much I loved doing them, but cycling was my true love. I told him about my cervical spine fusions and my fear of re-injury, but I was riding anyway.

He said, "You should do an Ironman. My brother is an Ironman coach. His organization is called VIP Endurance Coaching. Give him a call."

With an attentive expression on my face, I admitted, "I've

always wanted to do an Ironman. I just never thought it would be possible."

"Call my brother," he repeated.

I called his brother, Scott, and said, "I work with your brother. He suggested I give you a call."

"What can I do for you?" he declared enthusiastically.

"I want to do an Ironman competition," I eagerly responded. "Cycling is my true passion, and I have a lot of cycling experience. I have also completed several marathons and ultramarathons, but I don't know how to swim long distances."

He replied, "No problem. I'd be happy to coach you."

I signed up for my first Ironman Competition, Lake Placid Ironman, in 2016. I chose Lake Placid because it is my and Kristen's favorite town. Also, after Kristen and I were married, we went for coffee at a local café. All over the walls were posters and paintings of different athletes who had completed the Lake Placid Ironman.

I said to Kristen, "I've always wanted to do an Ironman."

She smiled and said, "I know you could do it."

The owner of the café overheard our conversation. He paused and laughed loud enough for me to hear. I could feel my ears burning. The old feelings of anger and embarrassment hit me, and I wanted to punch the guy in the face, but I didn't. Instead, I put "complete an Ironman" on my mental bucket list.

Scott prepared me well for my first Ironman, a 2.4-mile swim, a 100-mile bike ride, and a 26.2-mile marathon all in one competition. Kristen and our beautiful seven-year-old daughter, Hope, returned with me to Lake Placid, NY, to support me in my first Ironman outing.

We rented a campsite for Hope, Kristen, and I at a local KOA. I was nervous because I had never done an Ironman before. I was trying to set up my bike stand but it wasn't cooperating. "I can't get this stand to sit right!" I yelled.

My daughter gazed at me with her beautiful blue eyes and said, "Daddy, you can do anything. You're an Ironman."

Later in the day, we were sitting at the pool watching Hope swim.

Kristen began chatting with a lady sitting next to us, and the woman said, "We are leaving soon. We want to get out of town before the Ironman competition starts. It gets too crowded."

Kristen said, "Oh, my husband is competing in his first Ironman."

"Awesome! Is he going to get the tattoo?" the lady asked.

Kristen replied, "What tattoo?"

"Athletes who finish usually get the Ironman logo tattoo. Most of them have it placed on their calf muscle."

"Rob doesn't know anything about that," Kristen admitted.

After the lady left, I leaned over and whispered in Kristen's ear, "When I finish, I'm gonna get that tattoo."

The morning of the Ironman, I stood at the starting line with two thousand other swimmers, waiting for the cannon to fire. Boom! And we were off. Everyone hit the water.

Kristen later said, "You guys looked like a fish feeding frenzy."

I was not prepared for the insanity of hundreds of swimmers diving into the water at the same time. There was no room to swim. I could not get into the rhythm of my stroke and began to panic. It felt like I would drown.

Unable to catch my breath, I inhaled water and choked. To make matters worse, swimmers swam over top of me and pushed me out of the way. Someone's foot kicked me in the face, knocking my goggles sideways. I dog-paddled out of the mayhem to catch my breath. When I looked up and contemplated the crowd of swimmers, I said to myself, "There is no way I can swim 2.4 miles like this. I guess my race is over."

But something inside me would not let me quit, a stronger voice, and it told me, "You can't quit. It's just starting." I moved from the center of the swim space to the outside for more room. On the outside, the frenzy diminished, and I was able to find my rhythm. It took less than two hours to complete the swim.

When I left the water, two people stood there, ready to remove my wetsuit. I held up a finger and said, "Wait a minute." Then, I lay down and hugged Mother Earth. I was so happy to be out of the water.

They ripped my wetsuit off, handed it to me, and I ran to the bicycle transition station. At that moment, I knew that the rest was history because I was going to finish. I completed my first Ironman competition several hours later. Not only did I finish this one, but I also completed two more Ironman competitions, all three in Lake Placid, NY. And, yes, after my first one. I got the Ironman tattoo on my right calf.

My resume for endurance competitions was becoming extensive. I completed seven marathons on the road and more than fifteen fifty-mile ultramarathons, four of them at the Palo Duro Canyon, my favorite run. I competed in four one-hundred-mile ultramarathons: the Vermont 100 twice and the

Javelina Hundred twice. But the long-distance running was taking its toll on my body, and I wasn't sure I could keep up with training for ultramarathons. I began sustaining overuse injuries.

One day, a friend said, "Since you love cycling so much, why don't you try Endurance Cycling? It's not as hard on the body."

His comment made sense. Up to this point, I had been riding bicycles on and off for over forty years. Endurance cycling was new to me. I had heard about it but was more interested in professional cycling and one-day races. After doing research, I learned that endurance cycling meant learning how to stay on the bike for days at a time. It was about being equipped for the long haul, not so much for speed.

This was the time of the COVID-19 pandemic, and as a precaution, all endurance competitions were cancelled. If I was going to stay committed to endurance exercise, I would need to find something else. I reconnected with my love for cycling and thought about what my friend said. I started going for long bike rides. On one of my rides, I had a spiritual experience and just felt so grateful to be on my bike, feeling light and free. It was almost like the feeling I got when I first saw my brother riding his new racing bicycle down our driveway forty-six years ago.

I called my older brother. "Hey, Ben," I said when he picked up the phone. "I just wanted to call you and thank you for the gift of cycling. I went on my favorite ride today and felt so grateful to just enjoy a country ride."

Soon after that phone call, an ultra-cycling event, Race Across America (RAAM), crossed my radar. Every time I googled endurance cycling, RAAM showed up. My RAAM research began. I learned that I could not just enter the race; I had to qualify by completing one of their RAAM-approved races. I found a qualifying race in Alpine, Texas, called No Country for Old Men (NCOM). Because of the pandemic, the race was modified so racers could self-crew and keep human interaction to a minimum. Ben lived a few hours from there. I reached out to him again and asked him if he would be willing to support me.

Without hesitation, he said, "Yes. And I'll ask my friend James to help, too."

Not knowing how to compete in an ultra-cycling event, all three of us did our homework. We met up a few days prior and put together a plan. It was a 375-mile race with challenging elevations and insane winds. Many riders did not finish because of the wind and the climbs.

After the first one hundred miles, I said, "Boys. It's going to be an early night; my legs are shot!"

My brother and James gave me a funny look, and Ben challenged me, "What? You didn't come all the way out here to quit!"

I looked at him with a dumb stare on my face and said, "Yeah, you're right. I didn't come all the way out here to quit."

I got back on my bike and just kept going. I settled into a rhythm, and no matter what, I just kept going. After thirty-plus hours, I finished the race and placed fourth overall in the solo event, qualifying for RAAM.

Instead of jumping right into RAAM, Ben and I decided it would be best to do another trial race. We needed more experience. In June of 2021, Ben, James, and I were back at it. Only this time, we invited other friends to join the support crew—childhood friends Rod and Tim, my wife's best friend, Carolyn, and Ben's friend Cameron. We registered for an event called Race Across the West (RAW). It was a one-thousand-mile race from Oceanside, California, to Durango, Colorado. It ran along the same route as RAAM. We were all inexperienced, but RAW would provide us with the necessary experience to compete in RAAM. We started out in a three-day heat wave with temperatures exceeding 120 degrees. Rather than park the van and wait out the heat, we decided to get a hotel room about twenty-five minutes away. It was a lot of downtime, too much to make up. Hours later, we left the course again in search of a hotel room, creating even more downtime. After five hundred miles, the team came to the realization that it was mathematically impossible to complete the race in the allotted time. Instead of wasting energy, we strategically dropped out of the race. Although the entire crew and I were sad, we also believed it was a huge success based on the wealth of experience gained.

I have since come to realize that, to me, competing in endurance events is not about outcomes. I've had plenty of successes, and I have had plenty of disappointments—not failures. The beauty of training for an endurance event is that I go beyond my physical and mental limits, and I have to rely on support. I cannot be successful alone. All my life, I resisted help and stayed in safe mode. Max Lucado, a Christian author, described it as, "Tree huggers—People who are afraid to go out on a limb." Because of my background and my childhood trauma, failure always seemed inevitable. Ultra events force me to break down that barrier. Just getting to the starting line is success!

I no longer try to escape from my emotional pain but run and ride through it. I look forward to my ultra training and even enjoy running at 5:00 a.m. with a headlamp. Training sets me free. In the early morning quiet, I become a fullback for the Dallas Cowboys. I play third base for the New York Yankees. I become a professional cyclist, training with Greg LeMond and Steve Bauer. When I am training, I am a better husband, father, son, sibling, grandfather, Christian, and overall, a better human being. My spirit yearns for greatness, tapping into potentials I never knew existed. My endurance pursuits lead me toward that greatness. When I see a mountain, I want to climb it, to embrace it. Training allows me to show the world that there is life after trauma and abuse, a life beyond our wildest dreams.

My first Ironman, Lake Placid, 2016.

Ben, James, and me after the No Country for Old Men ultra bicycle race in West Texas. I finished fourth overall and first in my age group.

CHAPTER SIXTEEN

Life after Trauma

"There is no timestamp on trauma. There isn't a formula that you can insert yourself into to get from horror to healed. Be patient. Take up space. Let your journey be the balm."

- Dawn Serra

My next feat is to complete Race Across America (RAAM). I have retired from public service. Now, with my life experience, education, and the platform of endurance, I want to provide hope and healing for people who have suffered trauma and abuse—people who have nothing to lose. I want to show people who have suffered trauma that it is possible to follow your dreams and to be successful. I have been preparing my entire life to conquer a herculean feat, such as Race Across America. I want to conquer it like I conquered my fears. I am blessed to have the capacity to train full-time and organize our support team. Our team motto is "Believe."

I do not live a perfect life, but I do live a peaceful one.

No longer do I hang on to hatred and resentment. I have internal rest. I am a truly grateful human being. God gave me the gift of Himself, the gift of love, the gift of family, the gift of friendship, the gift of cycling beyond my wildest dreams, and the gift of knowing my true self, without hatred and pain. Life continues to challenge me, but the miracle today is that I no longer try to escape. There are still days when I want to hide under my covers and stay in bed. And sometimes I do. The beauty is, I don't stay in that place. Life is too precious. I face life's challenges with God as my director. And God always directs me to help others.

I start every day by asking God to direct my path. I ask Him to divorce me from self-pity and self-seeking motives. My only request is that He guide my thinking for the next twenty-four hours. I stay on guard against selfisÚess, dishonesty, resentment, and fear. When they crop up, I take care of them immediately. Although my stubborn, strong will still tries to take the reins from Him, I am now willing to give them back. Irritability, misery, and discontent are my allies when they make me realize that I am trying to be in charge. And when I give the reins back, God smiles at me and says, "I understand."

I adore and love my Roman Catholic faith. I attend Mass regularly, and I am a Lector at my local parish. Every day, I ask Our Blessed Mother to intercede for me. Mary, the Mother of God, has been with me throughout my life. I am forever grateful to Mrs. Leap, who left my prayer at the Grotto in Lourdes, France. When I attend Mass, seeing the altar reminds me that God's grace heals brokenness. And it's through the Eucharist that I can go out into the world to be a disciple of Jesus. My eyes and ears are always open for God. I want to be there to help someone in need, just like there were people sent by God to help me through the darkest moments of my life.

I am forever grateful for the people God sent to me. My childhood friend, Jackson, passed several years ago. He had an enlarged heart and didn't know it. He died way too young. My friend, Denis, passed about fifteen years ago. He died of sleep apnea, and I miss him so much. I want him to meet my daughter, but that time will have to wait. Mrs. Leap passed a few years ago as well. She will always hold a special place in my heart. My friend and sponsor, Roger, passed about ten years ago from lung cancer. I miss him and find myself wanting to talk to him when life gets difficult. Although many of my friends have passed, God continues to bless me with caring, loving people.

My dear friend Father Stan still gives me the plain truth, and I would not have it any other way. I try to live up to my Igbo name, "Chukwuemeka," God had done so much, by being of service to my neighbor.

I continue to practice the twelve steps and attend twelve-step meetings. At the time of this writing, I have been sober for thirty-six years. God, in His extraordinary wisdom, sent me another sponsor, an Irish Catholic from the Bronx. JoÚ and I talk every day. We share common bonds, recovery, and our Roman Catholic Faith. We practiced the Exodus 90 program, a spiritual roadmap to a stronger relationship with God through prayer, ascetism, and fraternity. It is designed to make us better men, better Catholics, and better Christians. It guided us with daily readings and reflections.

God blessed me with family beyond my wildest dreams. Kristen and I celebrate our marriage anniversary on October

8. Our daughter, Hope, is in high school and progressing well. I often think about when my childhood fell apart, leaving me with very little hope. And now I have lots of Hope every day.

My boys are all grown up with families of their own. My ex-wife and I are blessed with twelve grandchildren. Although we have been divorced for over thirty years, we are still friends and do our best to be good grandparents. Eight of my grandkids live nearby, and I get to see them on a regular basis. The other four live in South Carolina. I get to see them during special events and holidays. I am not the best grandparent, and I do make mistakes, but I am truly grateful that they have a grandfather who is not bogged down with addiction and the pain of the past. I'm a prankster, and my granddaughter often says, "Grandpa, you're a pest!" It brings me tears of joy because the alternative me would not even be around to enjoy her.

To this day, I love cycling, maybe more than ever. Most of the time, when I ride, I am one with the bicycle. I would never have imagined, when I first saw my brother riding his brand-new racing bicycle down our driveway, that cycling would see me through so many difficult times. But it did and still does. There are times I can feel myself wanting to escape the realities of life through training and long bicycle rides, but when I do, I recognize that my internal compass is off, and I must make it point true north, straight to God.

There is life after trauma. It is not an easy road, but with an open mind and the willingness to Let Go and Let God, there is a whole new way of life. I have learned that the key to unlocking the pain of the past is forgiveness. Forgiveness opens the door to letting go of toxic shame, guilt, and hatred and replaces them with God's love. The world becomes a much better place. Now, I am happy to be me, and I will spend the rest of my days trying to help others find themselves so they can, one day, be able to say, "I am happy to be me."

When I left the Caron Foundation, Rick, one of my counselors, handed me a piece of paper and said, "You have a tough road ahead, but just remember, you are not a chicken; you are an eagle." When I got to my car, I read the paper he gave me.

The paper described the story of a farmer who found a wounded eagle in his field. Not knowing what to do, he took it home and nested it alongside his chickens to keep it safe. He kept the eagle with the chickens and fed it and took care of it until the eagle began to heal.

One day, some visitors came by his place and saw the eagle. They asked the man what he was doing with an eagle in his chicken coup, but the farmer had forgotten the bird was an eagle. The bird stayed with the chickens so long that even the bird forgot he was an eagle. The farmer simply replied that it wasn't an eagle; it was a chicken.

The visitors encouraged the farmer to take the bird out and see if it could fly. So, the farmer did. And of course, the eagle was completely healed from his previous wounds, so he began to fly. Everyone watched as the bird flew with the magnificence that only the most elite of all flying birds could accomplish. The bird flew higher and faster than anything.

In many ways, I had been the eagle living in a chicken coop. I had become so used to having such low self-worth and low self-esteem that I just stayed down most of the time. It was my norm. I've since come to learn that I am not my abuse, and I am not my past. I am worthy of love, and I am a good person. And so are you.

For so many years, I believed my spirit was damaged and could never be repaired. I now know that God's love heals. It has been revealed to me that my spirit is not blemished; it just had calloused layers of protection covering it. I want the world to know that God's love *can* heal, "The caged bird sings because he has a song to sing." My bird is singing now, and it is free. It wants to bring hope and relief to trauma survivors. It's true, we can't ever be the same, but we can be healed. We can live amazing new lives. We can unlock the cage and soar to the highest heights. It is like a sweet melody to know our caged bird can sing again. It is as the Psalmist David wrote in Psalm 103:1-5, "I Bless the holy name of God with all my heart. Yes, I will bless the Lord and not forget the glorious things he does for me. He forgives all my sins. He heals me. He ransoms me from hell. He surrounds me with loving kindness and tender mercies. He fills my life with good things! My youth is renewed like the eagle's!" Let your bird sing again. I pray you find your eagle's wings and fly to the highest heights.

Acknowledgments

Writing this book has been somewhat of a paradox. It has been painful to relive trauma and to shine a light on some very dark memories. But the pain provided healing and insights. This book is not intended to drag anyone through the mud. In fact, I never wanted to tell this story. But because of the true friendships I developed on this journey of life, my desire to keep my story to myself changed. I am forever grateful that people close to me encouraged me to offer hope and comfort to anyone who has suffered trauma.

To my wife, Kristen, who had to endure the highs and lows of this process. For her care, moral support, and countless hours of editing. I could not have completed my memoir without her.

To my daughter, Hope for being patient with me on this roller coaster ride.

To my grown children. For enduring the hardships of being raised by a dad who had so many internal struggles to overcome. I am so proud of all of you.

To Made for Success Publishing, specifically Bryan Heathman, Alice Kirkwood, and the editors. Thank you for holding my hand and walking me through this process. Your kindness and support made all the difference.

To my mom, dad, and siblings. Thank you for your understanding.

To my brother JoÚ. Your acknowledgment of my pain of putting pen to paper without your own personal baggage attached to it opened a door I had shut. Opening that door led me to a newfound freedom.

To my dear friend and mentor, Father Maduawuchi (Father Stan). Thank you for always giving me the plain truth.

About the Author

Robert H. Woods is an author, speaker, accomplished endurance athlete, and retired educational administrator. He is a father of five and a grandfather of twelve. Robert holds a PhD in educational leadership, focused on transformative learning and synchronicity. In his athletic endeavors, Robert is inspired by athletes such as ultramarathoner Scott Jurek, ultra endurance cyclist Markoh Baloh, and professional cyclist Greg LeMond. As a survivor of childhood trauma and abuse, Robert's life ambition has been to offer hope, love, and support to children and adults who have endured the horrors of abuse and trauma.